WE KNEW
Paul

BOOKS BY MARIAN HOSTETLER

African Adventure
Fear in Algeria
Journey to Jerusalem
Mystery at the Mall
Secret in the City
They Loved Their Enemies
We Knew Paul

WE KNEW
Paul

Marian Hostetler

HERALD PRESS
Scottdale, Pennsylvania
Waterloo, Ontario

Library of Congress Cataloging-in-Publication Data
Hostetler, Marian, 1932-
  We knew Paul / Marian Hostetler.
    p.   cm.
  Summary: Several young people relate their encounters with
Paul, who traveled extensively teaching about Jesus.
  ISBN 0-8361-3589-X
  1. Paul, the Apostle, Saint—Juvenile fiction. [1. Paul, the
Apostle, Saint—Fiction. 2. Christian life—Fiction.] I. Title.
PZ7.H8112We 1992
[Fic]—dc20   92-10562
                                                              CIP
                                                              AC

The paper used in this publication is recycled and meets the minimum requirements of American National Standard for Information Sciences—Permanence of Paper for Printed Library Materials, ANSI Z39.48-1984.

When Scripture is directly quoted, it is from the *New Revised Standard Version Bible,* copyright 1989, by the Division of Christian Education of the National Council of the Churches of Christ in the USA, and it is used by permission. For references, see page 125.

WE KNEW PAUL
Copyright © 1992 by Herald Press, Scottdale, Pa. 15683
   Published simultaneously in Canada by Herald Press,
   Waterloo, Ont. N2L 6H7. All rights reserved
Library of Congress Catalog Number: 92-10562
International Standard Book Number: 0-8361-3589-X
Printed in the United States of America
Book design by Jim Butti/Cover art by James J. Ponter

00 99 98 97 96 95 94 93 92 10 9 8 7 6 5 4 3 2 1

To those many modern-day Pauls
who are cross-cultural sharers
of the good news

Contents

Preface, by Luke 9

1. *The Holy Terror,* by Simeon of Bethany 11
2. *The Unexpected Guest,*
   by Elizabeth of Damascus 21
3. *True Magic,* by Lucius Paulus of Paphos 31
4. *A New Life,* by Timothy of Lystra 39
5. *My View from Philippi,* by Euodia 49
6. *My View from Philippi,* by Syntyche 55
7. *My View from Philippi,* by Clement 63
8. *No Difference in Christ,* by Julia of Corinth 75
9. *The Fraud,* by Septimus ben Sceva 89
10. *Lucky?* by Eutychus of Troas 95
11. *Uncle Saul,* by Benjamin of Tarsus 103
12. *Neither a Murderer nor a God,*
    by Drusilla of Malta 115

Bible and Song 125
The Author 127

Preface

Dear Theophilus,

Greetings to your and to your family. I was glad to hear how much you liked the second book I sent you about the events which followed Jesus' return to the Father. You wrote to ask if I could write a third book and continue this account from where I had left off, with the apostle Paul in prison. I regret that at my age and with my physical condition, it isn't possible for me to undertake the traveling, correspondence, and research necessary for such a task. That will need to be left to others.

However, you also mentioned that your grandchildren are eager readers of my writings. By the way, how are they doing in their studies? Is Gaius still planning to study medicine?

When I heard of the interest these young people have, I decided to send you something which I hope will especially appeal to them. This is something I could prepare without extra research and travel, since

I had on hand a number of short manuscripts among those I had collected before writing my other books.°

From these accounts, I've selected some written by young people—that is, they were young when they met Saul—or Paul, as he was later called. Each of these stories gives a different glimpse into Paul's life and personality. You will no doubt recognize that I had already made some use of these letters in my own earlier narratives, but there was much more than I could use then. I have edited these stories to fit them together into a suitable whole, but I hope you'll still hear all of them speaking in their own personal ways. I've also arranged them in chronological order according to when these youths had their encounters with Paul.

I have many other stories, as well as my own remembrances of my experiences with Paul, but I've chosen these in the hope that they will speak to your grandchildren, and perhaps, God willing, to others as well.

Your friend,
Luke

° Now called *The Gospel of Luke* and *The Acts of the Apostles,* in the Bible.

1

The Holy Terror

by Simeon of Bethany

I met Saul only once and for only a few minutes. To understand how that meeting came about, I need to tell you first about my family's association with Jesus himself.

He was a great friend of my aunts, Mary and Martha, and of my uncle Lazarus. They were my father's sisters and brother, and we lived near them in Bethany. My father, Levi, was the oldest of the family, and he was the only one who was married. Since his parents weren't living, he felt responsible for his brother and sisters and was always thinking of how he could arrange marriages for them.

One time Lazarus told Father that when he was in Galilee on business, he had met a rabbi of that northern area. When Father learned that Lazarus was going to entertain that rabbi and twelve of his followers for dinner during their visit to Bethany and Judea, he wanted to meet them. Maybe among them would be husband material for Mary or Martha, I heard him say to Mother.

My parents and I were invited that evening, too. Aunt Martha always liked to have things just so, and she was rushing around, trying to be sure the meal was perfectly cooked and served. But Aunt Mary just relaxed and listened to the rabbi, Jesus, talk. She looked pretty sitting there, with her brown eyes glowing and her long brown hair falling in waves over her shoulders.

At first, Jesus wasn't too impressive. Yet, whenever he spoke, everyone listened. I soon began to feel that he was talking directly to me. However, when we discussed it afterward, I found out that everyone else felt like he was speaking only to them!

I don't remember much about the men with him, except that there was one who interrupted Jesus twice with his eager but not-too-intelligent comments. And there was another who kept eying the expensive old family tapestry hanging in the dining area and also the alabaster flower urns, as though he was estimating their value. Later I learned these two were Peter and Judas.

After that first time, the group usually stayed with my relatives whenever they came to Jerusalem for one of the feasts, since Bethany was nearby. My aunts and uncle thought there was no one like Jesus. My father said, "Jesus is an interesting man, but he has some unusual ideas. He's going to be heading for trouble. The priests don't like unusual ideas."

Then came the events which shook up our whole

world, and nothing was ever the same again. Ever since he was a young boy, Uncle Lazarus sometimes became very ill and would have difficulty breathing. No one knew what brought on these spells. (Probably an asthmatic condition worsened by allergic reactions. Luke.) This time he had a worse attack than ever, and before a week had passed, he died.

My aunts had sent for Jesus. They were hoping that he'd quickly come and heal my uncle, as he was said to have healed all kinds of other sick people.

Jesus did come, but four days too late. When he arrived, he wanted to go to the burial cave, so we went with him to show him the way. As we walked, he was crying and praying. When we got there, he told us to move the stone away from the cave entrance.

What a strange request, we thought. But Father and I together managed to heave the huge boulder aside.

Then Jesus called, "Lazarus, come out!"

And he did! Lazarus walked right out of the tomb, still wrapped up in the burial cloths!

Many who saw this believed that Jesus was the Messiah we'd been expecting. No one else could do such a thing as to call the dead back to life. It didn't convince our temple leaders, though. Instead, they began to plot to kill Jesus, and what's more, to kill my uncle, too, to destroy the proof of Jesus' power.

Things were so stirred up that Jesus and his disciples needed to leave Jerusalem quietly. But we weren't afraid. Now that we knew the power he had, we had only one question: When was he going to use it and become our king-Messiah?

Then the time came, we thought. Jesus had left Jerusalem secretly. Then suddenly, at the beginning of

13

the week leading up to the great Passover Feast, he came back openly. The crowds cheered him on his way as he rode a donkey from Bethany to the gates of the city. I was there, too, shouting praises to God and running alongside. I yanked a branch from one of the palm trees and waved it jubilantly. Yes, the time for Jesus to set himself up as our king had come!

But everything went downhill from there. In less than a week he had been arrested, tried, sentenced, tortured, and killed. It wasn't safe for the disciples to stay with us at Bethany, so they quietly scattered and sometimes met under cover somewhere else.

Only Lazarus, Martha, and Mary were not completely crushed and hopeless. As far as Jesus being a king-Messiah, yes, that dream was over. But might he not return as their friend?

Lazarus kept saying, "Jesus brought me back from death. He can surely do the same for himself."

Almost right away we began to hear a rumor that Jesus' tomb had been found empty, even though the governor had posted Roman soldiers to guard it. Another rumor was that some of his followers, women from Galilee, had seen him alive. We could hardly believe that, though. If he *had* come back to life, wouldn't he have come to Bethany to see his good friends?

Then one night a month later, Peter slipped in quietly and told us that it was true: they *had* seen Jesus several times. I didn't hear what more he said because I had to leave and take my younger brothers and sister home to bed.

I wasn't present either a few days later when the adults of my family, as Peter had instructed them, went to a hill outside our village. There they met a group of Jesus' followers who had come out from Jerusalem. I can only tell you what my parents said happened:

Suddenly Jesus was there with them, too! He explained to all of them that they were to be witnesses for him, apostles sent to spread the news that he was alive. But first they needed to wait for the Holy Spirit that he would send. In that way, although away from them, Jesus would still be with them. And then he disappeared in a cloud. And no one has seen him since.

A few days later, as he promised, this Holy Spirit came to 120 of his followers in Jerusalem. Through the Spirit's help, the frightened disciples turned into bold preachers. Peter, who at one time had been afraid to even admit that he knew Jesus, preached about him all over the city.

The result was that thousands believed the message that Jesus was really God with us, that he had died and come alive, and that, through believing in him, we could come near to God. My parents and aunts and uncle were among those thousands who believed and were baptized. And I believed, too, and went to some of the daily meetings. However, I was too young to be baptized at that time.

Even a number of the priests believed. But others became more and more upset; they were the ones who had plotted against Jesus and had him put to death. Once they arrested Peter and John, and later they arrested all the twelve apostles and put them in prison. When the priests were ready to question the apostles, they couldn't find them. They were no longer in prison, but in the temple, preaching! An angel had opened the prison doors for them!

But for the most part, things went along without too much trouble. Those of us who believed in Jesus continued to meet together and to sing and pray and share our food and money. But we were all shocked when Stephen was killed. He was a great man. He could heal people and could speak like an angel. Yet he didn't mind helping to do the humble things like serving the food at our meals together.

Stephen was so influential and such a convincing speaker that the religious leaders arrested him. They brought him to their council for a trial, like they had done with Jesus. In his testimony to them, when he downgraded the importance of the temple and their place in it, they became furious.

Then Stephen accused them of murdering the Messiah Jesus, who was now ruling in heaven with God. They were so out of their minds with anger that they forgot about needing the Roman governor's permission to put someone to death. They dragged Stephen out and pelted him with jagged stones until he died.

Father heard the news in Jerusalem and hurried home to tell us. But as it was, we didn't have time to worry or wonder about what this might mean for the rest of us believers.

Mother was still sobbing, "Oh, not Stephen, not Stephen!" when we heard shouting in the street.

Then there was a loud hammering at our courtyard gate, and a voice called, "Open, in the name of the temple guards!"

We ran to look out the door of the house, but before Father could decide what to do, the gate was bashed open. In came a band of five men, their clubs ready.

A sixth man that I hadn't noticed stepped forward.

He wasn't wearing a temple guard uniform, but was dressed in a long plain robe of fine linen and had a stole draped over his shoulders with fringes a foot long. Tied to his forehead and to his left arm were larger-than-usual Scripture boxes.

He must be an important Pharisee, I thought. He was rather short, but I soon forgot that because of his air of command and the fanatical hatred glaring from his eyes.

"You are Levi, the silversmith, and his wife, Anna?" he snapped.

"Yes, but . . . ," Father began to answer. The man interrupted. "You are under arrest for being part of this blasphemous sect which is trying to destroy our holy traditions.

"Take them with the others," he commanded the guards, and they seized my parents by the arms and began to march them out the gate.

My little sister began screaming, "Mommy! Daddy! Mommy!" till one guard slapped her and told her to shut up.

I followed to the gate, stunned, and saw more temple police out in the street, standing around Martha and Lazarus.

The Pharisee in charge turned back, looked straight at me, and said, "You're the oldest child. Your brothers and sister are your responsibility now. I hope you haven't been infected by this heresy. If you have, know this: it's going to be rooted out regardless of the cost. I have the responsibility to do this from the council and from God himself, and I shall fulfill it." Then they left.

That's how I met Saul.

Little Anna, Andrew, and Lucas were all crying and I nearly was, too. I was too shook up to be able to think what to do. We were too scared to go out to the neighbors, and when they saw what had happened, they were afraid to come near us. So we sat huddled together till night came and I lit one of the oil lamps.

As I was looking out the door, I saw by the moonlight a figure slip through the broken gate. The shadow came toward the room where we sat. It was Aunt Mary! She came in quietly and hugged each of us.

Then Aunt Mary whispered her story—that she had been in the garden when the soldiers came and had hidden in the tree she used to climb when she was a girl. Martha and Lazarus must have told them she was away, for the guards had looked around a bit but had not really searched.

"We must sleep now," she said, "and tomorrow very early, we'll take what food and clothes we can and go south to my uncle Reuben's in Hebron. We'll be safe there until . . . we can come back here and find my brothers and sister."

That's what we did. We made backpacks with some clothes and food. It was hard walking with the little ones, but after a couple of days we arrived in Hebron and were welcomed by my great-uncle Reuben.

Several weeks later, when things had quieted down in Jerusalem, Uncle Reuben began "pulling strings" and inquiring among his influential friends. He learned that Lazarus had become sick from being beaten and had died in prison. After a year my parents were released, with Martha.

Father's leg had been broken and had been left uncared for, so now he always walks with a limp. Mother is quieter than she had been before. Martha too. But they tell how some of their guards came to believe in Jesus.

And we've heard other stories about the believers who hadn't been put in prison but had fled and scattered. Wherever they went, they told about Jesus. Now there are more and more believers all over the country, instead of only in Jerusalem!

As for Saul, I've heard that he's changed. People say that now, instead of trying to destroy us, he's become one of us. I don't know if this is true. I suppose anything is possible.

2

The Unexpected Guest

by Elizabeth of Damascus

Three days ago Abner, the ruler of our largest synagogue here at Damascus, came to our place and showed my father the letter from Jerusalem. It had come from the office of the high priest, written by his secretary and stamped with his official seal. It said:

Caiaphas, the High Priest, to Abner of Damascus, Ruler of the Synagogue of the Street Straight; greetings in the name of the One True God of Israel.

We have been disturbed to hear that some of the heretics who follow the teachings of that executed criminal, Jesus of Nazareth, have come to your city and have been spreading their blasphemous doctrines in your synagogues.

Therefore, we are pleased to inform you that, at his request, Saul of Tarsus, our most devoted and trusted agent in the battle to exterminate these erroneous teachings, will be coming to you to carry on in Damascus the work which he has done so well around Jerusalem.

You will, of course, give to him (and to our temple guards accompanying him) every aid possible in his efforts to put an end to this heresy. I also expect you to supply him with the necessary hospitality. You will inform the rulers of the other Damascus synagogues. Our envoy Saul should be reaching Damascus shortly after you receive this letter.

"So, what's to be done, Abner?" asked my father. "And why are you showing the letter to me?"

"I'm showing it to you," replied Abner, "because I'm asking you to provide the hospitality demanded. You have the space in your house. And you're the one who usually provides lodging for any of our fellow Jews who come here on business, if they don't have any relatives here to stay with.

"As to what's to be done, I don't know. I think I'll let our friends who fled here from Jerusalem know what's going to happen. That'll give them time to go somewhere else, to flee again, if that's what they think is best."

"Be careful, Abner," said my father. "We've heard from these Jerusalem refugees what this man Saul is like. You could be in danger yourself if he should find out you have any sympathy for them."

"I know. Maybe here we're too far from the center of things, from Jerusalem, but I can't quite see what there is to get so worked up about. I'm not convinced that this Jesus really was our Messiah or that he came back to life, like these people believe. But neither am I convinced that we need to kill them or put them in prison. If it isn't true, they'll soon give up on it. Better to ignore them instead of making them so important!"

Then Abner added, "You'll need to be careful too, Judas, if Saul's headquartered here."

Father replied, "A fellow like him will be so busy trying to dig up dirt, he won't have any time for us."

"Yes, well, he'll dig wherever he can for information, and he might want to start right here with the digging," said Abner.

"So, Elizabeth," he turned to me, "you and your mother just be real sweet to him. Maybe he's such a cranky fellow because he doesn't have a nice wife and daughter like Judas here does."

"Well, I'll try to be nice," I said. "And I'll be careful, too. I've become friends with Hannah and Mary since they've been here. I wouldn't want their parents to be arrested."

What kind of person is this man? I wondered, *to make such a long journey just so he can drag people off to prison, people who hadn't done anything wrong!*

Our job in the next days was to prepare for this guest and the temple guards with him and to try to ready ourselves to be nice to him. I hoped he wouldn't find anyone here he thought deserved prison. Maybe my friends would decide to hide somewhere, because I was rather sure that if they were questioned, they wouldn't lie about their beliefs.

Three days after that letter arrived, at about 1:30 in the afternoon, the sun as usual was so burning hot that the streets and buildings seem to reflect back as much heat as glared down on them. This was the time when every person and animal found a spot of shade, indoors or out, and was resting.

Every normal person or animal, that is. But something abnormal was happening. I heard the noise of many feet in the street, a banging on the gate, the cry of voices. The rest of the family, too, was being roused from their sweaty slumber. It must be that man Saul arriving, so greedy to find some poor follower of Jesus that he had to be abroad traveling under the midday sun.

And it was. Here was our expected guest. Yet he turned out to be unexpected—not at all what we had been waiting for. He didn't come striding forcefully through the gate. Instead, two of the guards were leading him. His white robe was streaked with dirt, like he had been lying in the dust.

I had imagined that he would be full of words, rapping out questions and orders, making dogmatic statements. All he said was, "Please, I need a place to lie down."

Father looked puzzled but led them to the room we had prepared. As they passed near me, I saw Saul's eyes—they were blank, completely white! No iris or pupil was visible.

Soon Father came back with the two guards. He asked them, "Has the man had a sunstroke? You should know better than to travel at this time of day."

Father turned to Mother, "He should drink a lot of water, but he refuses to. Says he won't eat either."

The guards looked at each other. Then one of them said, "I don't know what's wrong. I don't think it's only a sunstroke. Maybe partly. It was very strange. We weren't far from the city, so he forged ahead and insisted that we continue on even through the heat.

"The sun was very bright, of course, but then suddenly there was a burst of light around Saul, much

24

brighter than the sun. He fell to the ground, like he'd been struck by lightning. And then it was like he went crazy. He was talking to someone who wasn't there! He called, 'Who are you?' "

"I heard someone answer him," interrupted the other guard.

"I didn't," declared the first. "You must have imagined that part. Anyway, after a few minutes, that brilliant flashing light went away. Saul got up, but he couldn't see anything, anything at all. I guess the light must have blinded him—but the rest of us, our eyes are okay."

"I, for one, had my eyes shut," said the second one. "It was impossible to look directly at that light. But maybe somehow, Saul did look and it blinded him. What do we do now? He hasn't given us any orders. That alone shows that something's wrong. He was always issuing commands before."

Father said, "I'll show you men where you can stay. All we can do is let him rest, and then see what happens." So they followed him outside to a roofed-over space along the courtyard wall, where they and the three other guards could tether their baggage donkey and spread out their bedrolls.

In the late afternoon, the sun's rays were at a slant and the heat had begun to be less intense. People begin to come alive again, and Father sent me to Abner to tell him about Saul's strange arrival. Abner came back with me, thinking he should greet the high priest's delegate, but Saul refused to see him. "I cannot talk, I will not talk to anyone now" were the only words he would say when Father informed him of the visitor.

25

Then it was evening. The air had a cooling gentle touch as it came through the open doorway and window. We were sitting on the floor for our evening meal. Cool cucumbers, the flat bread I had baked on a clay platter over a fire in the courtyard, grilled goat meat prepared as a special treat for our guest, and sweet golden melons.

Everything tastes so good, I thought, taking another piece of the garlic-flavored meat with my fingers and popping it into my mouth. *Why wouldn't the man eat anything?* I wondered again. *Or drink anything?* I took another sip of fresh grape juice.

Before we had begun eating, Mother had put small servings of everything on a reed tray for me to take to Saul's room. When I had quietly come near, I could hear him talking, praying it seemed. I thought I heard, "Oh, Lord God, oh, Lord God, I only want to serve you. Show me your truth."

Then there was silence. I tapped on the open doorway. "Sir, my mother sends you some vegetables, some meat and bread, some fruit. Won't you eat something?" I went and knelt by his bed. "Or drink some of this juice?"

"Thank you. But I will not eat or drink anything until I clearly know and understand God's will."

I took the tray and left.

• • •

That had been the first evening, a Tuesday. On Thursday it was the third day since Saul had arrived. His eyes were still blank, and he still refused to see anyone or to eat or drink anything.

The guards had soon become bored and restless and took turns visiting the markets and shops and who knows what other parts of our pagan city. There would certainly be sights different from Jerusalem for them to see—Syrian temples, Roman temples, Greek temples, all with their various idols and gods.

Father had gone out to our fields to supervise the beginning of the barley harvest. Mother had gone to do the daily marketing. So I was alone when someone knocked at the gate. It was a man I knew slightly, although he wasn't from our synagogue but from one of the others.

"This is the house of Judas, isn't it?" he asked. I nodded.

"I am Ananias, and I have come to see Saul of Tarsus."

"You may come in," I said, "but he refuses to see anyone."

"God has sent me to see him," Ananias answered. "I didn't want to come, because I've heard the evil things he has done, but I must obey. Tell him I'm here."

I went to Saul's room. "Sir, a man has come asking to see you. He says. . . ."

"What's his name?" Saul interrupted, speaking in an eager way I hadn't heard from him before.

"He's Ananias."

"Yes! He's the one God said he would send. Bring him here!"

Ananias followed me to the room and went up to Saul, hesitantly. Then he said, "Brother, the Lord Jesus who spoke to you on the road to Damascus has sent me to you. I didn't want to come, for I'm one of those followers of Jesus whom you've been persecuting. But the Lord has told me to. . . ."

"Yes, yes!" said Saul. "He told me that you would come to heal me and help me."

Ananias then put his hands on Saul's head and said, "In the name of Jesus, may you see again, and may his Spirit fill you, for our God has appointed you to be a witness for him."

Then the white coating over Saul's eyes melted away and uncovered lively brown eyes that looked eagerly around the room. "Praise God, I can see again!" he exclaimed.

"Fetch a bowl of water," Ananias said to me. Puzzled, I ran to do as he said. Was Saul at last going to drink?

Ananias took the bowl, and Saul knelt down on the mat. Ananias poured some of the water on Saul's head and said, "I baptize you in the name of the Father, the Son, and the Holy Spirit. Your sins are forgiven."

I had heard of such baptism. That was how those who wished to be part of The Way showed their decision. But I had never seen it. Then they embraced each other. They were both smiling, such smiles that it was like God was in them and shining out through their eyes.

Saul turned to me. "So you are the one who has kindly come to me with food and drink. I refused everything because I was fasting and waiting for God's will. Now I'll be happy to eat and drink anything you can find!"

I went quickly to find some bread and cheese, some wine and water. But all the time my mind was in a whirl. How could that happy, kind man be the same as the harsh and severe hunter of people we had heard about? The one who fanatically hated all people of The Way, had been baptized in Jesus's name!

Could this be a trick to find out who Jesus' followers were? No—these last three days couldn't have been acting or part of a plot.

I can't tell you all of the surprises of the next days. But there was no doubt, to us, anyway, that Saul was sincere. He went immediately to the synagogue on the Sabbath. Earlier he had certainly preached against Jesus, but now he preached for him. He told the people he had seen Jesus in that flash of light on the way to Damascus and that Jesus had spoken to him and set him on a completely new route.

Saul said, "Jesus is the Son of God!" He was now saying the very words that he had imprisoned and killed people for saying. Everyone was astounded at first. But his experience was so exceptional, his arguments so persuasive, that many were convinced, including my parents and me.

But the more who believed, the more hardened became those who didn't. Now it was Saul who was threatened with the same fate he had come to bring to others.

Two of the guards who came with him became believers. The other three deserted him, taking with them their copy of the high priest's authorization for imprisonment of all followers of The Way and giving it to Saul's opponents.

His new friends were able to hide Saul at first. Saul soon saw that he would be bringing danger on us, and he thought it would be better if he left. Before he could leave, we heard that his enemies were watching everywhere, especially at all the gates leading from the city.

If Saul showed himself anywhere, he would be captured and put to death. They were watching the exits from the city to prevent his escape. They also began to search one by one the houses of people they thought might be sympathetic to him.

Saul came back to our house temporarily. We hoped that because he had been with us before, they wouldn't search here, thinking that he wouldn't dare to come to so obvious a place.

Then we acted according to the plan dreamed up by Abner. Saul's Pharisee robe, fringed shawl, and turban were discarded, and his beard was shaved off. Disguised in the rough tunic and headcloth of a laborer, he went to the house of a certain friend.

The back wall of this man's house was also a part of the city wall. That night, by using a rope basket fastened to long cords, they silently lowered him from the window of the house to the ground far below, outside the city wall. We heard later that he arrived safely back in Jerusalem.

That's how I knew Saul.

3

True Magic

by Lucius Paulus of Paphos

My father, Sergius Paulus, is an important man. He represents the Roman emperor and is the governor of the whole island of Cyprus (148 miles from east to west and 40 miles from north to south). We live in the capital city of Paphos on the western end of the island. There are important copper mines back in the mountains covering most of the interior of the island, and other cities and ports are scattered along the coast.

From where our villa is perched on the hillside, I can see the deep blue-green waters of the Great Sea and watch the ships come and go. Some head west to Rome; others go toward eastern ports such as Sidon or Seleucia. Goods and travelers usually come and go by sea. There are trails through the mountains to the interior villages and mines, but most travelers and merchants use the quicker and easier water routes.

However, we recently heard that there would be several men arriving sometime soon by the land route. Soon meant any time from two days to a month or more. They were wandering Jewish teachers.

A number of Jews have been living on Cyprus for many years. They originally came from the southern part of Syria, from our Roman province of Judea and the region of Galilee. Mostly they keep themselves separate from us Romans and from the native Greeks. These Jews are very touchy about their god and consider him to be above our Roman and Greek gods, and even, it's said, above the emperor.

My father likes to learn about the customs and beliefs of the various peoples living here. Much of what he knows about the Jewish people and religion, he's learned from one of their leaders, Elymas. He calls himself a "prophet" of his people, yet he prefers to be known by his Greek name, Elymas, rather than by his Jewish name, Bar-Jesus. He claims to have magical powers.

My father has studied the Jewish religion a bit and says it condemns magic and sorcery. So he has some doubts about the information Elymas gives on the Jewish religion.

Elymas does seem to possess some sorcerer's skills, however. He has entertained us with such things as causing small animals and objects to disappear before our eyes, or making a flower or scarf appear from the air by a snap of his fingers. Other times he does frightening things like darkening the room and then bringing forth from the underworld horrible, ghostly voices and forms of the dead.

Anyway, Elymas was the one who told us about the

itinerant Jewish men, led by Barnabas and Paul. As they went through the island, they were stopping and preaching in every synagogue—the Jewish places of worship. The group started in Salamis on the east coast and was coming this way.

It's unusual, first of all, for there to be traveling Jewish teachers. But more unusual yet, Elymas reported that they've been preaching and teaching to anyone who would listen, not only to the Jews. If this is true, it's indeed something new.

I didn't think the Jews, at least the ones we know in Paphos, were welcoming people. They'll answer questions about their religion, but they don't try to spread it around. They almost seem to resent anyone else having an interest in their religion, which they say their god has given exclusively to them.

One morning I was with my father in the governor's office in the city. This is the building where he receives official visitors and messengers and where he judges any matters which the lower officials cannot handle.

Sometimes when there's nothing too important scheduled, he lets me observe the routine. "Who knows, one day you could be appointed to a position similar to mine, maybe even to a higher position. So listen and learn," he told me.

Yes, I'd like the power and prestige of such a position. But being with him on the unimportant days is often boring. This was one of the boring days.

I sat listening to the cries of peddlers from the street. "Buy your grapes here—good grapes, good price." "The best sandals made from the finest leather. You'll wear them forever. Sandals! Sandals!" I could hear a braying donkey and the creak of cart wheels, and nearer, outside our door, the steady tread of the pacing guards.

Father was reading some reports from the port tax assessor, and then his secretary entered and bowed. "Sir, Elymas the magician is here, asking for an audience with you."

Father put the reports aside. "Show him in, Tertius." Smiling at me, he murmured, "This should relieve your boredom for a bit!"

Elymas entered, bowing so low I feared he might knock his forehead against the marble floor. "Ah, Your Honor," he said in his too-smooth voice. "Thank you for your graciousness in receiving your humble servant." As usual, he wasn't dressed in the Jewish manner but was draped in the Roman style, with the folds of his flowing robe gathered together on his right shoulder.

"Greetings, Elymas," replied Father. "Welcome. I had been thinking of sending for you to inquire about something. But first, let me know *your* reason for seeking this audience."

"Certainly, Your Honor. You will no doubt remember that I spoke to you some time ago about the Jewish teachers traveling this way. I've been hearing more about them and their teaching. Since I was the one who told you of them, it's now my responsibility, I feel, to warn you.

"People I know from the towns they've passed through have told me that they're stirring up trouble along the way. They're bringing disgrace on innocent people like myself, people whose only aim has been to be grateful and law-abiding citizens under your rule.

34

"In fact, let me be so bold as to offer my advice, which you at times have been kind enough to listen to," he continued in his oily manner. "It would be better for this province and for *all* your subjects, not only us Jewish people, if you were to immediately deport them when they arrive, or at least to arrest them for questioning."

"Well, Elymas, you speak of the subject which I wished to discuss with you," said Father. "I too have heard something of their journey and teachings. I do *not* plan to take your advice, however.

"You know I'm interested in learning about people and their customs, in particular their religious ideas. We have often talked of these things. Therefore, I'm all the more eager to meet these men and to hear what they have to say."

"But, most honored sir. . . ."

Father didn't let him continue. "When they arrive in Paphos, no doubt they'll contact the Jewish community first. My request to you is that, as soon as possible after their arrival, you bring them to me at the villa, where the atmosphere is more informal than here. Do you understand?"

"Yes, of course, Your Honor. 'Your wish is my command,' as the saying goes. Certainly. I will inform you of their arrival and see that they appear promptly before you."

Although he spoke in this sickeningly agreeable way, I thought that underneath he was really raging and angry.

Several days later my father alerted us at home: that evening the traveling preachers would be with us. Many Jews will not eat in a pagan house—that's what

35

they call any house not inhabited by Jews. So Father told Mother not to have the slaves prepare a meal for the guests. If we found they were the sort who didn't mind eating with us, she could have some refreshments served later.

"Lucius, if you're interested, you may be present," he said to me.

Well, I didn't want to miss it and wondered how sly Elymas would behave in his unwanted role of having to act gracious to men he despised.

That evening two men entered with Elymas. The one I noticed first was tall, impressive-looking, calm, and at ease. The other man was shorter and filled with so much energy that it seemed to leap out through his flashing bright eyes and his vigorous gestures when he spoke. That's how we met Barnabas and Paul.

To tell you all they said would be impossible and pointless. You've heard these things from many other sources. It's enough to say that they told the story of Jesus of Nazareth, whom they called God's Son. They reported on his death by the Romans at the request of the Jewish religious leaders, and how three days later he had returned to life. Those who believed this (or believed "in Jesus," as they said), tried to spread this "good news" (so they called it). They wanted more and more people to hear and believe.

My father was quite taken with what they said. They were so convinced and so convincing, we couldn't help but be carried along. Father said, "To have a god who loves a person and who doesn't have to be bribed by gifts and offerings, one who by his spirit is beside you to help you—this is certainly a new idea and a most attractive one!"

At that, Elymas could no longer play his role of being agreeable. "Sir," he cried, "they are truly smooth speakers, but when one reflects on what they say, it's nothing but a pile of nonsense. I would go even farther. They come with smiling faces and lying words, trying to deceive you.

"Your Honor, you know the beliefs of our people, beliefs which our God has revealed and which we have followed for thousands of years. God is great, but there is also the one who is against him, the devil whom we also call the father of lies. I beg you not to listen to their insane and lying words!"

At that, Paul came and stood, facing Elymas. His voice was strong and relentless as he said, "The devil is indeed present here—in you, his son! You are the enemy of everything good, you who practice the kinds of magic forbidden by God. You are the one filled with lies and evil, trying to turn away into your crookedness those who would follow God's straight paths! And now God will show you his power which is greater than the magic of your master, Satan. You will be blind, until you wish to see God's light!"

Elymas gave a great cry. He turned his head from right to left, staring. "Light the lamps! What has happened to the lamps? Bring a torch!"

He reached out his hands and took a few faltering steps, stumbling against a brass lamp stand and nearly tipping it over. "Help me! I can't see!"

Father summoned a guard. "There's been a . . . an accident. See that someone accompanies Elymas to his home." Elymas haltingly left the room, guided by the servant.

Then Father turned to Paul. "I see you also have

magical powers, although you criticize those of Elymas. Wasn't that a rather drastic punishment for his words against you?"

"They were not against me, but against God," Paul replied. "I have no magical powers. The only power in me is the power of the Spirit of God. This blindness can lead Elymas to the light of God, if he is willing.

"I myself was like Elymas. I thought I was following God by opposing in every way our Lord Jesus. God had to strike me with blindness so I would listen to him and turn to follow Jesus. When I did, I was healed. Now I can see clearly, not only what the eyes see, but sometimes also what is in the heart. If I could be forgiven by God, so can Elymas. We must pray that it will be so."

"You have given me much to think about," said Father. "For a long time I've been interested in religious beliefs of all kinds. Now I've heard what I've been searching for, even though I didn't know I was searching for it. Can you please come tomorrow evening so I can hear more?"

It wasn't long until my father became a believer, a follower of Jesus Christ—or a Christian, as Paul said they were being mockingly called in Antioch. Paul and Barnabas then left us to sail over to Lycia and continue their job of spreading the good news.

As for Elymas, he never returned to see my father. We heard that after several months, his sight gradually returned. But he has never gone any farther from home than his own street. Though he has never again practiced his magic arts, he has also not become a Christian.

That's the story of how I met Paul.

4

A New Life

by Timothy of Lystra

In many ways my home was different from those of the other children in Lystra. Though my parents and grandmother loved me, I wasn't happy. I was the odd one, the one the others made fun of and teased. Why?

In the first place, my father was Greek and my mother was Jewish. Most people believe that religions and races should not mix, and both my parents' families, except for my mother's mother, would have nothing to do with us. My grandmother lived with us, but we rarely saw anyone else of either family, so I had no cousins for friends.

The Jewish children of our town would throw stones at me and shout, "Half-breed, dog. Half-breeds don't belong to God's people!" The Greek children didn't mock me as much, but they ignored me, convinced that they too were better than I was. Older people on the street would laugh at me. At least I thought they did.

Mother and Grandmother tried to persuade me that God loved everyone, and they quoted passages from the Jewish Scriptures which supported this idea. One of their favorites was Psalm 67, which says:

Let the peoples praise you, O God;
  let all the peoples praise you.
Let the nations be glad and sing for joy,
  for you rule the peoples with equity
  and guide the nations upon earth.

But that brings me to the second difficulty. There weren't enough Jews in our city for a synagogue school. My mother didn't want me to go to a Greek teacher and learn about false gods, so she and Grandmother taught me at home.

Many women don't know how to read and write, and if they do, they might perhaps teach their daughters, but not the sons. The fact that I was taught by women embarrassed me, and I tried not to let people know about it. Even though it was better to learn from them than to be ignorant, I cared—probably too much—what others thought.

Why didn't my father teach me? you may wonder. Being a Greek, he had not been instructed in the Jewish Scriptures. Yet he wasn't a follower of the Greek gods, either. Occasionally he used to go to the synagogue in Iconium, when business took him in that direction. But for nearly as long as I can remember, he hadn't been able to travel. He would sit in his chair. As his creeping paralysis got worse, he would lie on his bed.

I seemed to be sick often enough, too, with one thing or another. My mother always got an anxious look when I was ailing, probably afraid I might be getting my father's illness. I'll admit it's something that was often in the back of my mind too.

Thus I continued for seventeen years in this unhappy and lonely life, until the time of the events which I want to tell you about.

Though my family was somewhat isolated from the others in our city, even we began hearing some news that was being spread by means of traders and other travelers. The usual news source for us at Lystra was from the seaport of Attalia north to Antioch, then west to Iconium and a short hop south from there to Lystra.

The kind of news which arrived along this route was usually about crops in the surrounding provinces of the Empire—which were failing, which were doing well, and how prices were affected. Or it might be news about a new law proclaimed by Rome, or a new tax to be laid on us by them, or a new official appointed to our province. This time the news, surprisingly, had to do with religion.

There were, it was said, certain Jewish men who had arrived at Attalia and then gone on to Antioch. Nothing surprising about that. But what was surprising was what they preached: that back in Judea the Jewish Messiah had come, and that he had been killed by actions of the Romans and Jews together. Then, they claimed, he had come back to life and was now the Savior of everyone, Jews and non-Jews!

This teaching produced a great uproar in Antioch, and crowds flocked to hear their preaching. But there were some narrow-minded Jews who thought God's

41

love was for them alone, and they became jealous and stirred up trouble.

Many people, mainly Greeks (Gentiles, the nations, as Jews call the non-Jews), believed in this preaching. Well, in Antioch, the Jews are much more numerous and influential than here, and they got the important people of the city to drive out the visitors with their two leaders, named Paul and Barnabas.

Apparently they couldn't force them to be quiet, however. Next they arrived at Iconium, our neighboring city, and it was like a repeat performance of what happened in Antioch. The men spoke in the synagogue to large crowds of Jews and Greeks, and many of each believed. But there were many others, both Jews and Greeks, who were opposed to them. These opponents succeeded in forcing them to leave, with even more violence than at Antioch: they had plotted to kill them by stoning them.

That meant that Paul and Barnabas would either retreat and turn toward Antioch, or they would continue on. If they kept going on the main road, Lystra would be the next stop on their route. So the people of Lystra were excited, especially my family.

I was burning with curiosity. These men would be bringing a teaching for both Jews and Greeks. And for a person like me, half Jew and half Greek, it sounded wonderful. Perhaps at last I could find something to which I belonged. I would no longer be an outsider!

Even before they arrived, opposite parties were forming according to the advance rumors. Most were interested in hearing something new, and, notably among the Jews, others resisted anything novel.

Yet my grandmother insisted, "It's not new, that

God is for everyone. That's what our Scriptures have always said."

"Where will they go when they come here?" I asked. (I wasn't thinking *if.* They *had* to come here.) "We have no synagogue for them to preach in like they've done in the other cities. Couldn't we invite them to stay with us?"

"I'm not sure," said my mother. "I would certainly welcome them, but we're already disliked by some of the people of both sides. If they stayed with us, it would make it more difficult for the teachers to make a good start here."

They did come, but their first contact with Lystra was different from what anyone had imagined.

However, before they reached Lystra, my life was already changing. I had always avoided going out when I didn't have to. Now I was wandering the streets, and my wanderings usually took me toward the gate on the northern side of the city. At that point the road from Iconium entered town, and Paul and Barnabas would be traveling along that way when they came.

This gate was one of the favorite places for beggars. They could seek money from people coming into the city and going out. Here also people were carrying on their little businesses, trying to sell their small bunches of dried herbs or lentils or grain. Other people were there to visit with friends.

In addition, some stopped there to buy incense or flowers for an offering at the temple of Zeus, located on a small hill nearby, just outside the city. It wasn't a large temple, but it had white marble walls and eight marble pillars set in two rows on its porch. It looked pretty against the blue sky and the brown hills dotted with the silvery green of olive trees.

None of the people around the gate paid any attention to me, and I was beginning to realize that perhaps I had imagined some of the antagonism I had always felt from others. This particular day I became interested in watching a game that two men were playing. They each had twenty-four stones and tried to capture the other person's stones. I was so engrossed in the game that I didn't notice the two strangers who had arrived from the north.

"Greetings to you, citizens of Lystra," I heard a voice booming out in Greek. "We're travelers from the East, from Judea, and hope to spend some time in your city. I see from your temple over there that you are religious people. We too are religious. We're servants of the one true God, and we want to tell you about him."

It must be them, I thought, staring. The one who was speaking was small but energetic, and he talked with great enthusiasm. The other was tall and stately, watching his friend with a kind smile. All the people around the gate began clustering together, leaving their games and businesses. I could see more people who had heard the commotion hurrying from nearby houses.

I was so excited that I missed some of what the speaker said. (Later I found out that he was Paul.) But now I noticed that he was staring at one of the beggars. Perhaps I shouldn't say beggar. This man, Linus, had been born crippled. He always sat near the gate, and although he was truly needy (which many beggars weren't), he didn't pester people for money. Instead, he gratefully accepted what anyone gave him.

I was so near that I heard Paul say to him in a low voice, "I see, friend, that you have faith to be made well."

Then he said in a loud voice, "Stand on your feet!"

Linus jumped up and started walking around!

"It's a miracle!" someone cried. "The gods have come to earth, like they did long ago!" cried another. "The gods have come to earth, like they did long ago!" shouted several in unison.

Everyone in our area knew a story that ages ago a poor couple had given hospitality to Zeus and Hermes in disguise. Then these two gods had saved the couple from a flood which drowned neighbors who had turned away these strangers seeking shelter. The couple's house was turned into a temple. I discounted all this as a false legend—but many Greeks took it to mean they should worship Zeus to be safe.

Now someone went running to the nearby temple to inform the priest. The people began to go crazy with excitement. They even decided which "gods" had come to earth. Paul was the speaker, so they called him Hermes, the messenger god. Barnabas was tall and imposing, and they decided he must be the king of the gods, Zeus.

All this discussion was taking place in the Lycaonian language, and I could tell that the two men didn't understand what was going on. So I went up to them and translated for them what the people were saying.

"Oh no, this is the opposite of what we want," said Paul. "Healing is by faith in God. It is to help people look to God, not to the ones God has used to announce healing!"

But before he could say anything to the crowd, it

parted to make way for the temple priest. He and his assistants were advancing with chants and dances, leading two oxen and carrying huge wreaths of flowers.

"They're coming to make sacrifices to you as gods!" I quickly explained.

At that Paul and Barnabas became as excited as the shouting and rejoicing mob around them. "No! No!" they cried.

When no one listened, they began to tear their clothes, a sign of mourning and distress which everyone would recognize.

At last the people noticed their action and became quiet enough for Paul to speak to them:

"Why are you doing this? Stop! We are only human beings, like you! We've come to bring you good news. Turn to the living God, the one who made the heaven and the earth and the sea and everything in them. In the past God let all nations go their own way, although he has shown his kindness to you by giving you rain from heaven and crops in their seasons. God provides you with food and fills your hearts with joy."

Even with such words, he had a hard time convincing the people not to sacrifice to them. When the disappointed crowd had finally scattered, Paul turned to me: "We thank you, young man, for your help. May we know who you are?"

"I'm Timothy. My mother is Jewish, and my father is Greek. We've heard of you and have been hoping you would come to Lystra. We'd be very happy if you'd stay with us!"

I hadn't meant to say all that, I who was usually so timid and shy.

"And bring your friends too," I added, for by then I'd noticed that there were several other men with Paul and Barnabas.

"We'll be glad to come with you," replied Barnabas.

I led them through the streets to our home. We ate together, then talked for most of the night. Their words and the message they brought was for us like water falling on parched ground. The message seemed so true and clear and so suited to our needs.

This night was the beginning of a new life for me. Of course, one doesn't become a completely different person. Even now I'm still shy and don't have as good health as some. But I realize Christ's love and know that he strengthens me to serve him in the church.

At the beginning, although I admired Paul and Barnabas, I had no idea of how important Paul was to be in my life. He became of great help to me personally, like a father to me. (My own father died not long after the events told here.) I didn't dream that later he would choose me to be his assistant and eventually appoint me to be a church leader.

But all that is not what I wish to tell about now. It is rather to recount to you how I met Paul on his first long preaching trip for the Lord.

The visitors weren't able to stay long in Lystra. Their enemies from Iconium and Antioch arrived soon after they did, and they stirred up the same sorts of antagonisms as before. The Greeks were disappointed because Paul and Barnabas had been unwilling to be the gods they wanted them to be. And the conservative and closed-minded among the Jews were easily persuaded against Paul and Barnabas. So Paul's enemies from the three cities united against him and dragged him outside the city.

Near the same spot where some had wished to declare him a god, others now hurled stones at him.

They believed that they had killed him, but God's mercy and protection are great. We, his friends, found him alive, though unconscious. He soon recovered enough to limp into the city.

We were able to persuade him that he should leave Lystra. But rather than turning back, he and Barnabas went on to neighboring Derbe. Their work there was successful, with many believers and less opposition.

From Derbe they decided to retrace their route, so we had them with us again in Lystra. This time they did not openly preach, but met with the believers in our homes. They were appointing leaders and strengthening us to carry on in spreading the good news until they could return another time.

5

My View from Philippi
by Euodia

Yes, I'll be glad to tell you about Paul's first visit to our city. I've heard that some others have been asked to tell about it also. That hardly seems necessary since it was my mother and my family who were the first to welcome Paul and Silas and who became the first Christians of the city.

Let me first give you some of my family background. My mother is still an influential person in Philippi, the most important city in the province of Macedonia. I say still, because becoming a Christian wasn't good for her business. Her power and influence among the elite of the city isn't as great as it once was.

Even so, we have a high standing in society here. My mother, Lydia, is known throughout the region in business circles as "The Purple Cloth Lady." She has always been interested in religion. It has been, you might say, her hobby.

My mother's father began our business of dyeing, manufacturing, and selling the purple cloth used exclusively by the rich and famous. She grew up knowing about the business but not participating in it. My father was the one who made it his life, since my grandfather had no sons. Then Grandfather died at age sixty-eight. Soon after, my father drowned when the boat on which he was traveling was shipwrecked.

So my mother took over the business. She decided to move from Thyatira, where my grandfather had the business headquarters, to Philippi. Here we're near the sea and thus close to the shellfish from which the purple dye is obtained. Another plus is the easy access to the port and the main land routes for shipping our goods.

Although she was much taken with business matters, once the new workshops for dyers and weavers were set up, she had time to pursue her interest in religion. In Philippi she became acquainted with other business women with the same interest.

They were intrigued by the idea of there being one great God over all, rather than a myriad of gods—the god of war, the goddess of agriculture, the messenger god, the goddess of the moon, the god of the sea, the king and queen of gods, and so on and on. Of course, there's also the emperor from Rome who's been declared a god and whom we're all supposed to honor and worship.

Mother was attracted to a one-God idea taught by an ethnic group called Jews. Mother and her friends learned what they could from the Jewish men among their business acquaintances. But these men were not very open in sharing their beliefs. They also seemed to have the idea that religion was mainly for men. Why should women be so interested in it? And even more, why should women be running a business? To them, that was definitely a domain for men.

Mother and her friends would meet once a week along the river outside the city. They discussed their ideas and prayed to the God they thought existed but about whom they knew little.

The riverside was a pleasant place, one which had probably been used for years for religious gatherings of one kind or another. There were piles of stones here and there and several broken pillars—the remains of some long-forgotten temple. And the water was handy in case of need for any rites of purification.

Sometimes I went with Mother. I wasn't so interested in their religious discussions, but the grass and trees and peacefully flowing river were a relaxing change from the clamor and rush of the city.

Well, to our great surprise, one day as were meeting, there came four men, strangers, to join the group.

"I'm Paul," said the short, almost-ugly man in a bold voice. "This is Silas." He indicated his thin, bearded companion. "And here are Luke and Timothy."

Luke is the most handsome and intelligent looking of the four, I thought. But at the rear of the group, Timothy seemed so young and bashful. It would be fun to see if I could get him to notice me and to unbend a little.

"We've just recently arrived in your city," Paul continued, "and hoped that we might find a place of prayer here by the river. We've been sent by the one true God to tell about his love for all peoples. In a vision from this God, I saw a Macedonian man who said,

51

'Come. Come over to Macedonia and help us.' "

My mother immediately spoke up. "You've come to the right place! And surely the God has sent you. We believe there is one great God, and we've been praying that he would send someone to tell us more!

"Are you sure," she added with a twinkle in her eye, "that it was a *man* in your vision? You can see that we're all women here!"

Paul laughed, and he no longer appeared so unattractive. "Well, it was a Macedonian at least. Of that I'm sure!"

What they told us about the one God was not so different from what we'd heard before. But then, that wasn't surprising because we learned that Paul and Silas were Jews.

What was absolutely new was their report that this one God had come to earth in human form as the man Jesus. This Jesus, through his obedient life and his death and resurrection, is Son of God and now the way to God. If we believe this, then through the Spirit of God, we can have God with us and in us at all times.

"I could never have imagined such a thing," Mother said when they had finished speaking. "I thought it must be true that there is one great God. But how great that this God would want to be my friend and Lord! Yet it seems so right, so exactly what I need!"

Then as the other women left, she said to Paul and his friends, "This is my daughter, Euodia. She's heard what you've said, but could you please come with me and speak to the others at my home? There are my twin boys who are twelve, my old aunt, my business assistant and his wife, and the servants. They must all hear this good news, too!"

So they walked us back to our house. On the way I managed to find a place beside Timothy and was able to get him started talking. I learned he was from Lystra in the province of Galatia and that he had never been this far away from home before. Possibly he hadn't met any real city girls like me before.

Mother called everyone together in the inner courtyard. All the rooms open onto this space. One corner is used for cooking and washing clothes, but the rest is gardenlike, with two flowering mimosa trees shading the tiled floor. There's a pool in the center where gold carp flash among the water lilies.

This was our usual gathering place, since the rooms of the house were used mainly for sleeping. We sat on woven mats around the pool.

As the story was told again, everyone listened intently, even Titus and Timon, the twins. At the end, my mother declared, "I believe what you've said. I want to follow Jesus."

"Then we'll baptize you with water," said Paul. "Baptism is the sign which Jesus told us to use. It's the symbol of your decision and God pouring out his Spirit, and it makes you a part of the church."

"Do the rest of you believe? Do you want to be baptized?" asked Mother.

She was the head of the house, and whether they all believed or whether they decided to go along with what she wanted, I don't know. But they all said they believed, when Paul and Silas questioned each one. For myself, I think I believed, but I didn't yet really understand all that that meant.

So we stood around the pool, then stepped into it one by one, as Paul and Silas scooped up water from it and poured it over our heads.

The men went to the inn that night where they had been staying for the few days they'd been in Philippi. But then Mother urged them, "Please, you must stay in my house. There's plenty of room, and I want to share my home with you. It's very little compared to all you've shared with us."

So they agreed, and our house became the first church at Philippi. I was delighted to have Timothy around for a while so we could get to know each other better.

As the news spread, others soon became part of it, too, and the number of those who met and discussed and prayed together grew. You may hear about some of those believers from the others who write, but we were the first.

6

My View from Philippi
by Syntyche

I'm glad I was asked by my friend and doctor, Luke, to tell you my story. Euodia, of course, has informed all of us that she's been asked to tell what she knows. I think she tries to be friendly to the rest of us, but she's such a snob because of her mother's high standing. Outside her own family circle, she doesn't know too much about any of the rest of us.

However, my view too, is a personal one, as you'll see. My name at the time my story begins was not Syntyche, but Syene—the name, I'm told, of a town in faraway Egypt. I don't even know if this was my true name. Perhaps that's where my mother and I came from, I don't know.

My first memory is of sitting on the ground by my mother in a marketplace. I can hear the shouts and calls of the merchants, savor the aroma of the food being grilled to sell, and smell the odor of the animals for sale.

Then I see my mother, her body stiff and her eyes wild, saying strange words I can't understand. I see a fat, greasy man, his eyes bulging as he stares at her. Her words stop, her body slumps, and he places a silver coin in her palm and leaves.

Do I really remember that scene, or is it a compound of other dim memories? I know I was still very young when Mother made me watch carefully what she said and did with each person who came to her. Some came for magic potions to charm a lover or to curse a rival. Some came to ask for the future to be revealed, or to ask her to calculate by the stars the best moment for a marriage or for a business deal.

Mother told me the ways to judge people by the look in their eyes, by their clothing, by the way they held their bodies. From this she would know what to tell them that would please them, and would be able to say things that made them think she had secret knowledge of them.

As she consulted the spirits, her stiffened body and faraway look was all an act, too. But once or twice I wondered. Those were times when Mother was faint and pale afterwards and refused to say more than that she had seen a vision from somewhere beyond. Otherwise, I found these things easy and fascinating to learn.

She showed me how to make concoctions and potions. They weren't made from exotic things, such as a lizard's egg or the eye of a sea turtle or the hair from a zebra's tail, as she let people think. Instead, they were a mixture of common ingredients: dust, chicken bones, beads, and other things, sewed into small leather pouches.

However, she did have some special items in mysterious glass vials which she seldom used and which she wouldn't tell me about. She only said, "The others are make-believe—these are real."

This "education" of mine took place as we wandered from city to city, nameless in my memory. I was too young to have any sense of place or geography. I don't know where we were when my mother sold me. I don't know why she did it. I understood nothing.

I only knew that some men gave my mother money, and they took me away from her. "It'll be better for you," she said. "Just do for them what I've taught you." I was about seven years old at that time.

The two men who were to be my owners for eight years explained nothing to me. They bought me a new robe. It was white and embroidered with strange symbols and heavenly signs. Then we got on a ship and after two days arrived here in Philippi.

Other slaves were in the house where they took me. I learned that each one had a task to do to make money for the masters. Some had been purposely crippled or blinded and were taken every day to their special places to sit and beg.

Some, from little children to innocent-looking old women, were skillful thieves and could snatch a purse or its contents without the owners ever knowing till it was too late. They were also responsible for providing us slaves with food which they stole from the stands in the markets.

Still other slaves were beautifully gowned girls who had rooms to which they lured the men of the city. It was better yet if they could lure travelers, for these they could rob as well as seduce.

I was the first of a new project our masters were going to try—fortune-telling, talking to spirits, and practicing magic. For all of us, the aim was to bring money to our owners, and the beatings were severe for any who didn't produce as much as was expected.

I hated these men and feared them. But I liked doing the things I'd learned from my mother. I found that most people would believe anything. They were eager to pay for the nonsense I would say and the false charms and amulets I would produce. Inwardly I laughed at them all.

One thing I didn't like was when someone wanted to talk to the spirits of the dead or consult evil spirits. I soon found that though I tried to pretend, as in the other things I did, I couldn't. Something seized my mind. Sometimes I wouldn't know what I said or did. Other times I would be aware, but without any control over my actions or words. It became like a blackness spreading through my mind.

But my masters were very pleased. The things I said and did when in this condition apparently both frightened and attracted people. They were willing to pay a lot for these messages from the spirits. But I felt like I was becoming smaller and smaller, and that soon there would be nothing left of the real me. My body would be there, but my mind would be taken over by the darkness.

One day as I was walking through the city, I noticed three men and a youth with them. They paid no attention to me, but I called out, "These men are servants of the Most High God. They are telling the way of salvation!" I could hear myself saying the words, but what they meant, I had no idea. I followed them, repeating the same words over and over. They tried to ignore me and went on their way.

Again the next day I saw them and followed, crying out the same words. That day when I returned home, my masters were furious. "Why are you wasting our time? For two days you've followed these men and haven't brought back any earnings!" They beat me with leather straps.

My aching body kept me from sleeping, and I lay there and wondered at the meaning of the words: "Most High God. . . . salvation." The only power or god I knew was evil and condemning, not saving.

The following day, I went to another part of the city, hoping I wouldn't meet these men, but there they were, and there I was, following them once more and once more shouting the same words.

Then the shortest of the three men turned to me. He stared at me, an angry look on his face. Then he commanded, "In the name of Jesus Christ, come out of her!"

I felt a tearing sensation throughout my body, as though my very brain and heart were being ripped apart, and then, before I lost consciousness, it seemed like a soothing light spread over the wounds left by the departing darkness.

When I became conscious, I was lying in the shade of a canopy at the edge of the market area. I recognized the man sitting by me as one of the men I had been following.

"I'm Luke, a doctor," he said smiling at me. "How are you feeling now?"

"I feel . . . like I've been broken and put back together, but not in the same shape as I was before. I feel light. I feel free. Where is the man who spoke to the darkness in me? I want to thank him for sending it away!"

"His name is Paul. And we serve the Most High God, as you've been saying. But we knew you were not saying it because of God. The devil also recognizes that God exists."

"This Paul said 'in the name of Jesus.' What does that mean?"

Luke explained to me a bit about Jesus and God. Suddenly, I couldn't concentrate any more. I felt exhausted, and my mind became troubled again. "Oh, what will happen to me now? I can't work like I did before. My masters will kill me!"

He took my hand, "You mustn't be upset. Relax and let God continue to heal your mind and body. If you can listen calmly, I'll tell you what happened while you were unconscious. You may not realize that your unconsciousness lasted several hours."

I made an effort to rest.

"Your healing caused quite a stir. Your owners were soon on the scene. Apparently they're often around to keep an eye on the activities of their slaves. You were lying so still that they accused Paul of killing you. He informed them that you weren't dead but recovering, that you would never again work for them as before, and that they would never again make money from you."

"Oh, wonderful!" I clapped my hands.

"It's not so wonderful for Paul and Silas," he said. "Your owners dragged them off to appear before the judges of the city, accusing them of creating a disturbance and of advocating unlawful practices. I stayed here to watch over you."

"But what's happening to them?"

"We'll find out later. I'm not too worried. I know Paul has been in worse situations than this before."

(I'll leave it to Clement to tell the outcome of Paul and Silas's arrest.)

As for me, that's when my life really began. The magistrates took me from my masters and gave me my freedom. This was their way of punishing my masters for falsely accusing Paul and Silas and for leading the magistrates to unlawfully beat a Roman citizen, Paul.

(Sorry, Clement, but I needed to infringe just a bit on your story!)

Later, when I was baptized, I took the name Syntyche, meaning "Fortunate." Every day I give thanks to God through Jesus for the salvation I have (which I earlier had spoken about without knowing what it was). I thank God for the healing by Paul and Luke through Jesus' power. And I thank him for the new work I have, with Luke's help and teaching—that of caring for the sick and the old of the church, when they need such help.

Indeed, I am Fortunate.

7

My View from Philippi

by Clement

My father's job was unpleasant and dangerous. He had been a Roman soldier, but after his leg was injured, he could no longer continue in the army and was appointed to run the prison here in Philippi. One of his major concerns was to keep the prison in good repair and to be sure it was escape-proof.

The main reason for this was that Father, as chief jailer, was responsible with his life for each prisoner. If one escaped, Father would be killed for failing to perform his duty. Since the house our family lived in was next to the prison, we too were glad to have the prison in good shape. We felt safer that way.

My father saved money by not hiring an assistant but having me do the job instead. I kept the records—wrote down the name of each prisoner and the date he was brought in by the police, and beside each name, the reason for his being committed to prison.

Most were either thieves or those who drank too much wine and got into fights. Sometimes there were merchants accused of cheating, or people suspected of stirring up rebellion against Rome. In my records I also was to note the punishment prisoners received from the two Roman magistrates and the date of their release (or death).

Then I needed to keep a record of our expenses: repairs to the building; the salary of the man who once a week emptied the slops and swept out the accumulated filth; the wages of the night guard and the day guard. There was no expense for food. Usually the prisoners had friends and family to bring them food—from which we took a portion, if it was any good. Sometimes they needed to pay us money to buy food for them. Or they did without meals.

Of course, they had to pay more than the food was worth when we bought it for them, and we kept the difference. After all, we had things to do other than running around to buy food and other conveniences for the prisoners, such as oil for light, wine for drink, or water for washing—we supplied nothing like that.

Most of the people whom the police brought us from the magistrates were sorry-looking creatures—filthy and unkempt, bloody and bruised from their beatings, and maybe sick from them too. We didn't beat the prisoners unless they were insolent or complaining fellows. It was the magistrates who had the police beat them, either to get them to admit their crimes or to punish them for their crimes. Or both.

We also had nothing to do with deciding who was

innocent or guilty. Father's only job was to imprison those who were sent to him and keep them until he was told otherwise. I didn't think much about the creatures, other than to despise them for having become the garbage they were.

The prison was built something like this: with three barred doors to go through to reach the inner room. This inner room was reserved for any especially dangerous prisoners. Each room was equipped with iron chains, stocks for the prisoners' legs, so that they had to sit with their feet through the stocks and their arms held by the chains.

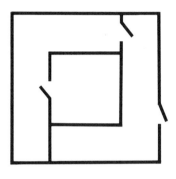

It was midafternoon one day when I heard shouting in the street. The sound was coming nearer. *Oh—more prisoners arriving,* I thought and was on my way from the house even before I heard my father calling, "Clement, get yourself over here!"

I could tell at once there was something unusual going on. For one thing, the magistrates had come along with the police rather than just sending the prisoners. As I've said, they're the judges, not we. But everyone knew they weren't particular about being fair, and bribes were helpful if you could afford them. So the fact that they were so involved as to come to the prison themselves made me wonder.

The next thing I noticed was the prisoners. Their clothes had been torn, and they had been severely beaten. Their faces were bruised, and blood was running down their backs. The rods the police were carrying were bloody, too. The men didn't look at all like the other prisoners we usually received. Their expressions weren't brutish or sullen, but calm and kindly.

The chief magistrate huffed up to me and said, "Write down Paul of Tarsus and Silas of Jerusalem. Jews who have disturbed the peace of our city. They have stirred up the people and have advocated unlawful practices and rebellion. They have each received 29 lashes with rods. See that they are kept in maximum security."

"Of course, Your Honor," said my father as I busily wrote down the magistrate's words.

"Who are the complainants?" I asked.

"Uh, Artemis and his partner, Fabius," was the reply. "These men have also seriously injured one of their slaves."

I looked up and, yes, there stood those two crooks, looking well-satisfied. Everyone knew about their schemes and the dishonest stunts they made their slaves do. I wondered how much they had paid out in bribes to the magistrates for this.

I finished my ledger entries, and followed my father as he and a police guard led the two men to the inner room. I looked at Father. He shrugged his shoulders as he saw my glance. Like me, he didn't think they were dangerous criminals, but he had to do what his superiors expected.

The prisoners had to sit on the floor and extend their legs to be locked into the stocks. Then their arms were chained to the wall. It was an excruciatingly uncomfortable position. For the first time, it began to dawn on me that prisoners were people like me. I began to wonder what it must be like to be shut up in the dark, half dead already from the pain of the beatings, and then to be shackled in such a way.

Instead of cursing us as we were locking them in, one of them called after us, "Go in peace. God bless you!"

"These men are strange, Father. What do those words mean?"

"I don't know," said Father uncomfortably. "I don't like it, but . . . what can I do?" he said as if to himself.

We ate the supper that Mother had prepared. My two younger brothers, my two older sisters, and I were seated with my parents on mats on the veranda, where it was cooler. The cooked grain spiced with garlic and cummin, the cool melons, and the grapes were delicious. But the food stuck in my throat when I remembered those prisoners, bound and chained, wounded, with no care, no food, nor anything to drink.

Later we finished eating, and Mother and my sister Sala had begun to carry away the platters. Just then we heard sounds coming from the prison.

"Go and listen. See what's going on," Father said to me. "I'll come if it's necessary."

I went and stood close to one of the barred windows. It was small enough and high enough that no one could escape through it even if they could somehow remove the bars. I had never heard sounds like these I was hearing now. It was some kind of singing, coming from the inner room. The melody caught my attention. The words, although I didn't understand their meaning, sank into my mind:

God loves us. He's our Savior.
God loves us. In him we live.
God loves us through his Spirit.
Through God's love, we can forgive.

God loves you, loves each person.
God loves you, though you sin.
God loves you. Won't you love him?
Now's the time you should begin.*

The other prisoners were completely silent. They didn't shout or curse as they usually did if one of their number stayed awake and made noises which kept them from sleeping.

After they finished singing, the two prisoners began talking. As I listened, I realized they weren't talking to each other, or to the other prisoners—they were talking to the god they had sung about.

Talking to a god! Was it possible to do such a thing? If there were such a god, why would he listen to a human? Yet the words of the song ran through my mind: "God loves us. . . . God loves you. . . ." If that were so, it would perhaps be possible to talk to him.

I went back to my father and tried to explain to him what I'd heard. It didn't make sense to him either. But he said, "Oh, well, as long as it doesn't cause a disturbance, we'll let them be."

In the middle of the night, I fell off my bed and woke up to feel the whole earth shaking. I'd felt the earth tremble before, enough to set a chair to jumping or to shake my mother's cooking pot, but this was an immense rocking.

---

* See page 126 for the words and melody.

I dashed outside for fear the house would crash in on me. But once outside, I stood frozen, fearful that the earth would crack open and swallow me. I saw that all the rest of the family had fled outdoors too.

My father was gazing dumbfounded toward the prison. My eyes followed his stare, and I saw that the prison's outer door was open, swinging on its hinges. Part of one wall had collapsed, and we could see the chains, still attached to the broken wall, but no prisoners were attached to the chains. Beyond that, in the darkness was a black hole instead of the wall of the inner room.

"This is the end for me," muttered my father in despair. He ran to the house and returned with his old army sword. Now he was ready to take his own life rather than to face the disgrace of having it taken from him. In the eyes of the law, he had failed his duty and let the prisoners escape.

A torch, still burning in its socket on the front wall of our house, must have lit the scene enough for the prisoners to see what my father was going to do. A voice shouted from inside the prison, "Stop! Don't harm yourself! We're all here."

The sword fell from his hand, clattering to the stone pavement. "Clement, get the torch!" Father said in a trembling voice.

I ran for it. By dodging among the fallen stones and climbing over the larger piles of them, we could enter the part of the prison still standing. The flickering torchlight revealed an incredible sight.

There sat all the prisoners, even though their chains had loosened during the quake. They could easily have fled during the excitement and terror. Somehow we knew they hadn't because of the two men in the inner prison. We also realized that it had been one of those two who had called out to my father.

Father went to them, full of fear, and bowed down. "Sirs, I see that the gods are very angry because you've been imprisoned, and yet you've spared me. Tell me, what I must do to appease their anger? What must I do to be saved from their wrath?"

"You need to know about Jesus and believe in him, and you and your family will all be saved and know God's love."

Father led them outside to a safer place. Everyone from our house gathered around to see these men who had been protected by the gods and who could protect us also.

That's what we thought—until we heard the words of Paul and Silas. They explained about the one true God whom we can know and serve through Jesus. Now I began to understand the words of the song I had heard them singing. It was not difficult to accept their words; we ourselves had seen the actions of God that night. We all believed what they said.

"Now, please give us the baptism you told us about," my father said. He sent a servant to bring water from the large clay jar in the cooking area.

"No," Father said when the water arrived. "This isn't right. First, let me use water to wash your wounds." And my father, who had cared nothing about any prisoners before, took a cloth and cleansed the wounds they had received from the beatings. After that, as water had washed away their blood and dirt, they used water to wash away our sins.

As another sign of the changes which had come into

our lives, Father then brought Paul and Silas—prisoners!—into our house, and Mother and my sisters prepared what food they could find in the middle of the night and served them.

My father was so happy. He thought of nothing else but helping these two men who had brought us such joy and good news. Yet, I couldn't help being worried. I whispered to him. "They're still prisoners, though. And what about the others?"

My father was dismayed and his joy fled. The short, dominant one seemed to know what I'd said to Father. This was Paul, whose voice had cried out to stop my father, and also, I remembered, who couldn't sing very well.

This Paul stood and said, "Silas and I will go and sit in what remains of the prison for the rest of the night. The others will also. They won't leave. You need only to wait to see what word comes from the magistrates in the morning."

The sky was already beginning to pale in the east as they went back and made themselves as comfortable as possible among the ruins of the prison.

In the early morning, two policemen came with a message from the magistrates, "Let those men go."

The police added their own message, telling us, "That earthquake was a strange one—it didn't damage every part of the city—only the area around the magistrates' homes and office, our police barracks, and here! The magistrates are scared and worried!"

Father went happily to tell Paul and Silas. "You were right. Word has come to release you. You can go in peace."

To his surprise, Paul said, "No. We will not leave in

secret. They beat us in public, they tore our clothes, they threw us in prison without any good reason. This they've done to us who are Roman citizens! Let them come here now and release us publicly. As for the other prisoners, perhaps they've been put here unjustly, also. At any rate, they haven't fled so they should be released too."

The police officers went back to report these words to the magistrates. Before long the two magistrates, dressed in their magisterial togas, were making their stately way to the prison. What fun it would be to see these proud, hard, and unsympathetic men needing for once to admit that they were wrong!

"Sirs," they said to Paul and Silas, "be assured that we didn't know you were Roman citizens. You have our apologies for any small inconveniences you may have suffered."

Paul said nothing.

"Sirs, please, you are free now to leave the prison, and . . . uh . . . free to leave our city. We feel you would be, uh . . . happier in some other place."

Paul then gestured to the other prisoners and spoke on their behalf. Since they were all there for petty offenses and the magistrates wanted to win back the regard of the people, they asked Father to release them as well.

We later learned that the magistrates were severe with Syntyche's owners. They tried to put the blame on Artemis and Fabius for not giving correct accusations and for not informing them of Paul and Silas's Roman citizenship. That's when the magistrates also gave Syntyche her freedom.

My family had gained our freedom too—freedom

from the darkness of lives without God. Father rebuilt the prison, but it wasn't the same as before. There were no chains or stocks. Each prisoner was supplied with a mat to lie on and simple food, and the sick or injured were cared for.

All these changes cut down greatly on the money we received, but we were never in need and could even share our money later on when the church sent gifts to Paul to help him in his journeys to spread the good news.

8

No Difference in Christ

by Julia of Corinth

Paul's been an important person in my life. I well remember our first meeting at Corinth. I was sixteen at the time. Not too long before, my parents had come here from Rome when Emperor Claudius had forced all Jews to leave there.

Corinth had the reputation of being one of the most wicked cities in the Empire as well as one of the most important. But we had lived in Rome, so Corinth didn't seem especially big or evil to us.

It was a struggle for us to arrive as refugees and to try to begin a new life. We weren't completely on our own, though. Like nearly every other city, Corinth had a Jewish quarter, and Father chose it over other cities where we might have located, because he had a cousin, Rufus, living here.

Rufus put us up until we could get our tent-making

business under way. He also lent us enough money to buy the first batch of camel and goat hair we needed to make a new start. We were able to purchase the looms with the money we had from selling the old ones in Rome, since they were too large to bring along with us.

I was glad when we moved from Rufus's house to our own place, even though it was small and crowded. The front room was for the weaving and sewing workshop. This opened onto the street, so it also served as a shop from which to sell our goods. Behind it was a courtyard for cooking and eating and all the other household tasks. Above the workshop was our sleeping room.

You might wonder why I was glad to leave our cousin's comfortable house, a mansion compared to our present place. Because of Rufus's son, Hiram. For me, any place that didn't have Hiram was better than any place that did. He liked me, but I didn't like him.

Hiram wasn't ugly, he wasn't fat, he wasn't stupid. But also he wasn't interested in anything beyond his father's business (sandal and shoemaking and other leather crafts), he didn't have a sense of humor, and he didn't like women to have much to say.

My mother, Priscilla, is the opposite of that. She has her opinions and is willing to give them. I think I'm like her in that respect. Since I could tell that Hiram didn't exactly approve of her, why did he like me? I was pretty sure he had already talked to his father about the possibility of our engagement. His mother wouldn't have been included in the discussion—she didn't count! So I wholeheartedly approved when Father found this small place for us to be on our own.

76

Ours was a family business. Father ran the work-shop. Mother did the purchasing of supplies and the selling. I did the housework and helped with the weaving when I had extra time. Tent-weaving was usually boring—everything all one dark dull color and no pattern. But occasionally someone wanted one with some patterns and varying shades. That I enjoyed more.

The day we moved in, I painted on the newly white-washed outside front wall in Greek: "QUALITY TENTS BY AQUILA AND PRISCILLA—in stock or made to order."

The only drawback was that we were still in the same neighborhood as Hiram, and he began stopping in nearly every day. I tried to make sure I was busy with the housekeeping or out marketing when I thought he might come.

Then came a day that turned out to be memorable because of the people it brought into my life. We were all in the shop, Mother doing accounts, Father and two men sewing, and five of us at the looms weaving. Then a stranger entered. This was not so remarkable, as most people of the city were still strangers to us, but he was an attractive young man, I thought. He had a remark-able proposition for our business.

"I'm Markus," he said, "business assistant to Titius Justus. You may know him. He lives next to your syna-gogue and worships your god."

Father said, "I don't know him, but then, we've only been in Corinth a few months."

"Anyway," Markus went on, "one of our main jobs has been purchasing and supplying everything need-ed by the Roman legion headquartered here. That's

5,000 men. They're not all here in Corinth, but this is the supply center for all of Achaia.

"The commander of these men, Antonius, has learned that he's to lead an expedition to regions in the north. There will be 2,500 new men coming here. Polus is a new commander who will remain here, while Antonius goes north with the 2,500 new men and 2,500 of those already here. Now, what we need is 1,000 tents before spring."

Everyone had stopped working and was listening with wide-eyed surprise.

"I'm not interested in going and bargaining with every tentmaker in the city," he went on. "I want to reach an agreement with one, and that one can, in turn contract out to the others. Of course, it's too big a job for one workshop. Are you interested?"

I could see he was a bit surprised when it was Mother who spoke up. "Yes, we are. But I need to know more specifics as to size and quality and price. And I need to have two days to contact the other tentmakers before I can sign a contract. Let's sit down over here and talk."

"Julia," she said to me, "please bring us something to drink."

I hurried out to the courtyard, glad that I had prepared some pomegranate juice the day before. To it I added some cool water from the stone jar. Then I put the clay pitcher and cups on a tray, along with some honey-dipped meal cakes.

When I returned with the refreshments, Markus stood and said, "Please join us, if your mother doesn't mind?"

He glanced at her. I could tell that she was surprised, but she nodded her assent. I sat with them but was too excited to do more than nibble on a cake.

"There may be something you'll enjoy doing with this order," he said. "Your mother says you prefer weaving when there's something colorful and original. Antonius himself has expressed an interest in having something more unusual for his own tent."

I didn't know what to say or think. He must have asked Mother about me! She would never be discussing what I liked or didn't like to do otherwise. And how else would he even have known that we were mother and daughter? I could have just been a servant.

I was in such a daze, I didn't know what else was said until I realized he was standing to leave. He was saying, "I'll check back in two days then to see what you've decided after checking with the other tent-makers. I hope to see you both then." And he was gone.

Mother gave me a look and said, "You can take the tray away now . . . and then get back to work."

"Yes, Mother," I said, and although I walked carefully and quietly with the tray, I felt like skipping and singing!

But that wasn't the end of the day's surprises. In the early evening, after the workers had left and we were beginning to close up, another stranger arrived. Not young and handsome this time, but older and rather ugly. His feet were dusty from travel, and he looked weary, as he heaved the pack from his back to the floor.

"Welcome, stranger," said Father. "You seem to be of our people. Where do you come from?"

"That could be a long story," the stranger laughed. "My name is Paul of Tarsus. Just now, I've come from Athens. My work is to serve our God by bringing good news to our people and to others as well, the news that the Messiah has come, the Messiah for whom we've been waiting so long."

He had certainly captured our interest with those words! But before we could comment or ask questions, he waved his hand and said, "But first, let me say that I've come to your home because I also am a tentmaker, and I need to find work. I must support myself along with the preaching and teaching I can do on the Sabbath and in the evenings. Would you have any work for me, and can you recommend a place to stay?"

"God has led you here, friend," said Father. "Just today we've had what will probably be a huge order for tents, and we'll need all the workers we can find."

"Yes," added Mother, "there's plenty of work, and we're also very interested in what you say about the Messiah. As for lodging, we have only this room and the one above it. But you're welcome to sleep in the shop here, or in the courtyard when the weather is good. And you may share our food as part of your wages."

"Fine, fine," he said. "I've learned to be content in whatever situation I find myself."

I led him to the courtyard where he could have water to wash himself. Then I finished preparing the bread, spicy stew, and fruit for our evening meal. Meanwhile, my parents closed up the shop, arranged the materials for the night, and prepared a corner where Paul could sleep.

We sat around the remnants of the cooking fire, our

faces half-shadowed and half-lit by the flickering light. As we ate, Paul began telling us about Jesus of Nazareth. He said this Jesus was the Messiah and God's Son, who had died and then was resurrected as the Savior for all peoples!

Paul could answer every question or doubt, because he had experienced them all himself before he had been shown the truth. I think that already that night, we were nine-tenths of the way to being convinced.

The next day Paul began to work. In and out of the thick tent fabric, his fingers were forcing an iron needle threaded with a strip of tough leather. Bone needles were too fragile for this work and snapped in two after several stitches. But the work didn't keep him from talking, and soon the workshop was filled with theological discussion.

I was surprised that what he said was not so clear and believable to everyone as it had been to us the night before. In fact, I could soon see some stiff opposition forming, especially from Joseph and Levi, two other sewers.

Joseph waved his needle in Paul's face and said, "You've been deceived by some vision from the devil! You were right before you *thought* you heard that voice. The Messiah is for us Jews only, and he'll do away with the Romans and be our ruler in Jerusalem!"

"I can't say things like I want to," added Levi, "but you come along to the synagogue on the Sabbath, and our teachers will set you straight."

"Of course, I'll come to the synagogue," said Paul. "I always go there first to bring the good news from God. But, like here," he looked around at the people in the shop, "not everyone will listen."

However, opposition didn't quiet him, and he kept on talking, telling stories about the life of Jesus that he had heard from those who had known him personally. Paul's way of speaking was such that no one could help listening to him, regardless of how much they disagreed.

Mother missed all the discussion while she was out making the rounds of the other tentmakers. In spite of the interest I had in listening in on the lively exchanges of opinion, I didn't forget that the next day Markus would be back.

The next morning I was wishing I could wear my new robe, the sea-blue one that complimented my dark hair and blue eyes, but I knew I didn't dare. What would Mother say? Instead, I put on the nicer of my two workday robes. It was an off-white, of finespun linen. I brightened it up by knotting at my waist a multicolored sash I'd once woven using remnants of red and blue yarn.

The first person to come in was Hiram. But I didn't dare leave for fear that Markus would come while I was gone.

Hiram's eyes lit up when he saw me. "You look nice, Julia." Then he frowned. "Why didn't your parents tell us about this Roman army business? Surely they'll need footwear, too. We want to get our part of the action."

Just then Markus came in.

"Is that him? Introduce me to him." Hiram pulled me along. I was embarrassed, but decided it was better to do as he wanted than to make a scene.

"Excuse me, sir. This is my cousin, Hiram. He and his father do leather work, and he wishes to meet you."

Hiram bowed. "My family would be honored to supply your needs for footwear."

"I'm afraid that's been taken care of already. I think, however, there may be need of some more leather-covered shields and perhaps some canteens. I'll let you know if that should be the case."

But Markus's attention was not fully on Hiram and his request. He seemed to be listening with one ear to Paul and the other workers, carrying on their discussion which had begun yesterday.

"Who's the worker with these new ideas?" he asked me.

"Yes, Julia," said Hiram. "He sounds quite radical. Your parents shouldn't allow him to disturb the others' beliefs—or their work."

I ignored Hiram's unrequested opinion and told Markus about Paul's arrival and something of the teachings he brought. "Perhaps Titius Justus would be interested," I said. "Paul will be at the synagogue on the Sabbath to discuss these things."

"I think he'll be interested. I am myself," Markus said as he went to join the discussion while waiting for Mother to come. Hiram trailed along, his face expressing disapproval.

I know I'm supposed to be telling about Paul, not giving my whole life story, but it all fits together, as you'll see. However, I'll summarize the next few months to get to the point of my story—a decision important to the church and to me personally.

Paul argued in the synagogue, trying to convince everyone, Jews as well as Greeks attending, that the Messiah was Jesus. Some Jews believed, like our family and Crispus, a ruler of the synagogue. So did some

Greeks, such as Titius Justus, Markus, and Stephanas. By then Paul had been joined by two traveling companions, Silas and Timothy, and the three of them went to stay at the much-larger home of Titius Justus.

In spite of the leader's belief in Jesus, there was intense opposition within the synagogue. Paul no longer argued and taught there, but began to use Titius Justus's house as a meeting place. But to his Jewish opponents, it was even more provoking to have him next door and openly competing with them.

During this time, Markus kept calling and checking on the progress with the tents, each time managing to speak at least a few words with me. We also saw each other every Sabbath at the open meetings at Titius Justus's house, and at the other times when the believers gathered there for prayer, teaching, and sharing.

One evening at the end of a meeting, Markus told me he would come to our house and speak to my parents about marrying me—if I was agreeable to the idea! You won't be surprised to hear that I didn't say no!

Shortly after my parents and I reached home, he was at the door. "Come in, Markus," said Father. "It's not the tents this time of night, is it?"

"No, not at all. I think you have learned to know me through our business dealings and through the meetings of the believers. I have no family here to speak for me, although Titius is a distant relative and has agreed with what I wish to discuss with you. He assures me of my position with him, so that I feel I won't have a problem in supporting a family."

My father was looking puzzled. "I see we've been even more discreet than I realized," laughed Markus.

"I would like to marry Julia, and she feels the same about me."

"Father, Mother, isn't it wonderful?" I cried, almost dancing with joy. Then I suddenly became aware that they weren't looking delighted.

"I didn't know this was going on," said Father, "or I would have discouraged you before things came to this point. The thing is, we have another person in mind for Julia. We've already had some discussions with my cousin Rufus. . . ."

"No! Not Hiram!" I cried. "You know I can't stand him! And besides. . . ."

"Julia, that's enough," he said sternly. "This hasn't been finalized, but regardless of that, you must know, Markus, that we Jews are strict about whom we can marry. It's very important that we marry only someone of our own religion."

Markus was looking grim. "Am I mistaken then, sir? I was under the impression that we *were* of the same religion. Are we not all Christians?"

Mother entered the conversation. "Well, yes, we all believe that Jesus is the Savior. We believe what Paul has taught us. But . . . there are great differences between us. Naturally, we want Julia to marry someone of her own kind."

"Mother, Hiram isn't even a believer. He and his family. . . ."

"Of course he believes. All Jews believe," said Mother. "Maybe he doesn't yet understand. . . ."

Markus interrupted, "Maybe *you* haven't understood. Jesus is for everyone. The church here in Corinth had left the synagogue, although not because it wanted to. You are no longer part of the synagogue.

When it was time to choose, you chose to go with the Christians, didn't you?"

My parents nodded. "But we're still Jews. We didn't give up our beliefs."

"I think we need advice," said Markus. "Will you at least agree to talk this over with Paul and others from the church?"

"Yes," Father and Mother agreed. "That would only be fair."

So Markus arranged it, and within two days we sat down together—Paul, Silas, and Timothy, along with Titius Justus, my parents, and myself. Markus had asked that at least one other non-Jewish Christian be present—Titius Justus. I insisted on being there because my life was involved, I had some power of decision since I had decided to be a Christian, and I had the example of my mother as a woman who was a responsible person.

Silas opened the meeting by saying, "I understand that Markus and Julia wish to marry and feel that they, although Greek and Jew, are both Christians, and so should be able to marry. Julia's parents, Aquila and Priscilla, think cultural and religious differences make it better for their daughter to marry a Jew.

"This is doubtless a problem which will occur many times in the church, so the decision we come to here, under God's will, can be far-reaching."

Paul spoke next. "Really, it's better to remain unmarried, as I am. An unmarried person is far more free to do God's work and go wherever he calls. However, that's evidently not the discussion now!" Everyone chuckled.

Timothy spoke up next. "My mother was Jewish, my

father, Greek. This made my childhood difficult. I felt I didn't belong anywhere. I loved both my parents, but I wouldn't choose this kind of childhood for anyone. Yet, I realize the case we're considering is somewhat different. These two wish to marry and are of the same religion. This was not the case with my parents. Still, they're of different backgrounds and cultures."

"I disagree," said Titius Justus. "This family is Jewish, yes. But they have never lived in Palestine. They have always lived in the Greek world. They speak Greek. The only difference has been in the practice of religion, and Markus and Julia will have the same religious practices."

Paul spoke again. "We Jews are taught from infancy that we are God's chosen people, his favorites for all time. Now, God has sent me to the Gentiles with the gospel. He told me so, and I believe it and teach it—that Jesus Christ is the Savior for the whole world.

"Even so, I always go first to the Jews. They are my people. I long for them to be saved. And always, to my delight, some believe, like this family here. (He pointed to us.) To my despair, many refuse, and like here at Corinth, I am rejected by the synagogue. I love all my brothers and sisters in Christ, but because of my birth and upbringing, I can't help but especially love those of my own race.

"However, the church of the future will be composed of those of every tribe and clan and people and language. It will be beyond the feelings of race and kindred that still bind us of this first generation. In Christ there is no longer slave nor free, male nor female, Jew nor Greek. We are one in him. We must begin to forget all those things which can separate us, and begin to think of those which unite us. There is one Lord, one faith, one baptism, one God and Father of all. Markus and Julia are among the first of this new people of God."

What more could anyone say?

And what more can I say to you? So my husband and I have been thankful to God and to our Lord Jesus Christ for his servant Paul and for the blessings that have been brought to us through him.

9

The Fraud
by Septimus ben Sceva

(This text is quite different from the others, but I include it, for I think it gives a good picture of Paul, in spite of itself. The title is also appropriate, but in a way that the author had not intended. Luke.)

I'm most happy to write about the fake teacher, Paul. So many have been impressed by him. The opposing (and true!) view should be expressed too.

My family and I met him in Ephesus. But let me first explain who we are. My father, Sceva, is a Jewish high priest. We are, of course, of the tribe of Levi, and we have lived in many places throughout the Empire. Once we even traveled back to the "homeland," to Jerusalem. There my father went to visit the priests at the temple.

Father was not even granted an interview by the so-called high priest! Some underling told Father that we were not of the true Israel and should not be doing our work of priesthood and exorcising demons. We sell charms and spells and curses (to keep away evil spirits), and we perform incantations (to call upon the good spirits).

But what do those Jerusalem priests, provincials who have never left their city, know about the wide world beyond their temple walls, the world in which nine-tenths of us Jews have lived in the centuries since we were captured and taken away from the homeland?

Our people have synagogues in every city for teaching, but the synagogue leaders are usually not of the holy tribe of Levi, let alone descendants, as are we, of the great high priest, Aaron. Thus we travel about to bring to our people some special additional access to the Almighty, beyond what the synagogues have to offer.

My six brothers (Primus, Secundus, Tertius, Quartus, Quintus, Sextus) and I, the youngest, have been taught all the special knowledge which our father had inherited from his father, and so on back many generations. Some Jews, who don't know better, accuse us of ignoring what is in the Torah or books of the law by Moses.

We say, "You can hear the Torah read in the synagogue every Sabbath. But you will likely have no other opportunity to experience the ancient priestly practices we bring to you and to have at your disposal the priestly powers of direct descendants of Aaron, powers which the synagogue rulers do not have."

When we arrived in Ephesus, we were ignored! All the talk was of a teacher and worker of miracles named Paul. It was said he had first argued with the synagogue leaders, talking about a Messiah he claimed had come.

They soon kicked Paul and his rabble-rousing followers out, so he had gone to continue his arguments in a lecture hall. This is where he still was, trying to convince everyone of his fantastic ideas. Furthermore, he was spreading these ideas among the Gentiles as well as the Jews.

(Well, of course, *our* services are available to Gentiles too, if they wish to purchase an amulet or a curse tablet. But our sales, or I should say the *help* we offer, is mainly for our fellow Jews.)

We wanted to know what we were up against. We needed to plan a campaign to get rid of . . . or rather, to display our superior teachings, so my brothers decided to send me to spy out one of his meetings.

So, there I was one evening, in the crowd at the Tyrannus Lecture Hall. It was a mob composed of all kinds of people: old and young, men and women (why weren't *they* at home?), rich and poor, Jew and Greek. Even some slaves. And they all listened attentively to this odd little man expound his even odder ideas.

I couldn't make much sense of what Paul said: Jesus this and Jesus that, in the name of Jesus, being saved, loving each other. Even the questions people asked him didn't make sense to me.

I went back and told my brothers and father that I couldn't see what all the fuss was about. "It'll soon pass away," I said.

"Oh, yeah?" said Primus. "He's been here doing this nearly two years now. I don't call that passing away. We should've sent someone with *intelligence* to check

91

him out. Secundus and Tertius, what did you find out when you talked to the people about him?"

"One thing is that he actually *works* in his spare time as a tentmaker!"

We all laughed.

"And," Secundus continued his report, "people claim that if a handkerchief or other cloth that he has used to wipe away the sweat while working touches a sick person, he'll be instantly cured. Or if it's spirits, they come out of the person touched by such a cloth."

"Wow!" said Sextus. "With no curses or spells cast? Wonder how that works. How much does he charge?"

"Nothing, you nitwit!" said Tertius. "Why do you think we're so concerned? Who's going to pay *us*, when Paul does it for free? And besides, the evil spirits really come out, they say. Not like the act we put on."

"Maybe we should leave Ephesus and go somewhere else?" ventured Quartus.

"It won't do, boys," said Father. "You know that in Philippi and Corinth we had problems drumming up business—and this Paul had been active in those places too. I think there's a connection.

"We may have to adapt some of his techniques to get the people's interest. We need to investigate a little more closely exactly what he does. Maybe our methods need to be modernized. They've come to us unchanged through many generations."

So our scouts, Quartus and Quintus this time, followed Paul around for a few days, and then came back to report. "We didn't actually see him do any exorcisms," said Quartus. "I guess he does them privately, but by pretending we had a sick brother and inquiring around, it seems like he does it by using the name of this Jesus that Septimus said he's always talking about."

"Yeah . . . he said something like 'do everything in the name of Jesus,' " I said.

Well, as luck would have it, the next day a woman came to us and said that her husband had an evil spirit. She asked us to cure him of it. So we dressed ourselves in our seven purple robes trimmed with gold embroidery and the seven matching turbans, lined ourselves up from the oldest to the youngest, and solemnly marched down the street, chanting—always an impressive sight, if I do say so myself.

As we entered the house, a shiver of fear went through me. Something dark and unusual was hovering about us. The man himself was sitting quietly, but his unblinking eyes had a terrifying glare.

"Here he is," said his wife. "Sometimes he goes wild and tries to destroy everything in the house. I've had to send the children to my mother's. And sometimes he sits like this and will say nothing."

"We're going to get rid of that evil spirit," pronounced Primus.

Then, just as we'd practiced, we all chanted together, "I command you by the Jesus whom Paul preaches, come out!"

The man slowly rose.

"It's working!" I thought.

His mouth opened, and a harsh voice spat out, "Jesus I know, and Paul I know. But you—who are you?"

Then he swung his fists, he jumped on us, he kicked, he scratched. He had the strength of ten men. Our turbans were flying through the air. His hands ripped my gorgeous robe from my body. Then he slammed me to the floor! Soon he had torn the clothes off all of us and flung us around the room like rag dolls.

Our only thought now was escape. As we stumbled and staggered out the door and down the street, his demonic laughter echoed after us. We limped away as fast as our bruised and bleeding bodies could go.

The next few days we hid in the inn while our sore bodies began to recover. Father was in a fury. He went out the first day, but he didn't stay long. He said that people were laughing at him and us, and that this incident was turning even more people to Paul.

The next thing we heard was that apparently Paul, that practicer of magic with his magic sweat-soaked rags which cured all ills and with his magic incantations, was now preaching against magic! And the people were so gullible that they listened to him! They even brought their books about magic and sorcery and burned them on the street—hundred of precious parchment scrolls worth fifty thousand pieces of silver!

But we knew he did his work for the devil. We heard that evil spirit cry out, "I know Paul!" before he injured and nearly killed us, the sons of a high priest.

That's why I call him "The Fraud."

As soon as we were well enough, we left Ephesus.

10

Lucky?

by Eutychus of Troas

My name means lucky or fortunate. But how lucky is it to always be pointed out as the one who fell—fell asleep and fell out the window? And I'm not sure why I should be asked to write about Paul. After all, I was unconscious during most of my association with him! Still, you can certainly say that I had *firsthand* contact with him!

It came about this way. I don't have any parents. They and my little sister all died in an epidemic when I was four years old. Since then, I've lived with my father's brother, but living more like a servant than one of the family. I didn't get an education like my cousins did. However, when I could manage to get away from my work, I sat with the others and their tutors, and so I learned what I could.

My specific job was to take care of the plants in the

various inner courtyards of my uncle's large house. There were trees for shade, trees and shrubs for flowers, and trees and vines for fruit.

I had learned from old Crypton, the gardener, all he knew about the care of each one—how much water and sunlight it needed, how each one reproduced itself, how each needed to be cut back and pruned for the best growth. Now I did most of the work myself. Crypton could manage to do only a few hours of slow work each day because of his gnarled fingers and stiff legs.

I enjoyed seeing the lemons, oranges, grapes, and peaches swell and ripen. Then their yellow, orange, deep purple, and rosy peach colors would glow like jewels among the green leaves.

I loved the hot brilliant hues of the red, orange, and pink bougainvillea, hibiscus, oleander, and flamboyant, brightening every corner. Each blossom or branch made an unforgettable picture against its background of cloudless blue sky or gleaming whitewashed wall. In cool contrast were the blue and violet cascades of the jacaranda and wisteria.

Gardening was not all beauty and enjoyment, however, for my aunt was particular. There was the never-ending task of picking up or sweeping up every fallen twig, petal, or leaf and transporting them out of her sight to the compost heap behind the servants' quarters.

As I grew up, I became more and more frustrated. I didn't belong anywhere—not with the family nor with the servants. In the evenings I began to roam the streets of Troas. In the mood I was in, it was probably fortunate that I had no money to spend, or I'm sure I would have spent it on drinking or games of chance. The people I saw guzzling and gambling seemed to be having fun compared to my lonely existence.

One evening one of my uncle's slaves, a fellow about my age named Dicius, said to me, "Eutychus, would you want to come with me to a meeting? Uh . . . I think you might enjoy it."

I usually tried to hold myself apart from the slaves. I might be a nobody, but at least I wasn't a slave. "Why should I want to go to a gathering of slaves?" I asked rudely.

Dicius flushed. "It's not just slaves. There'll be all kinds of people. It's . . . well, it's a religious meeting. Have you ever heard of Christians?"

I said I hadn't.

"If you don't mind my saying so, I've noticed that you . . . uh . . . don't have many friends and often go out alone. What can it hurt to come along with me once? You don't have to stay, and you don't have to go again if you don't like it."

I had never much noticed him before. Now I realized he spoke well, better than I did. He was only trying to be friendly, and I really had nothing better to do, so I agreed to go.

Here are my first impressions of that meeting. There were all kinds of people, like he'd said—including some pretty girls (well-watched over by their mothers). Some people looked even wealthier than my uncle. Others looked like they had arrived from begging in the streets.

Those who knew some songs sang them! I had never sung a song in my life before! There was one I liked which they taught us, about "God loves us. He's our

Savior." The melody kept bouncing through my head afterwards.*

Another thing: everyone talked to God, all at once, each one telling God thank you and asking him for favors. I just listened to Dicius. I could see there were others like me who were new and looking around, wondering what was going on.

Then a man, a leader of the group, talked and explained about the group ("church" he called it) and about Jesus. After that people just sat around and talked to each other. Dicius introduced me to the ones he knew.

Everyone was friendly to me. I didn't know how to react to such friendliness. They didn't know (or care) if I was a servant, a slave, or a regular person. They just seemed to be interested in *me*.

I was intrigued and went again. And again. I was gradually learning more and beginning to understand about Jesus. I went to the fourth-day meetings, which were especially for new people like me. These meetings were for learning about the faith and for discussion. And I went to the meetings on the first day of the week, where there was more singing, prayer, and teaching.

Then one fourth-day evening, there was great excitement. A group of traveling teachers of the church had arrived. Timothy, Gaius, and Sopater were the ones who talked to us that evening. Through their words things became even clearer to me, and now I knew that I believed, too. But the biggest news was that the greatest teacher of them all, Paul, was to teach

---

* See page 126 for the words and melody.

us the evening of the first day, before they all continued on their way to Jerusalem.

But when the first day arrived, I wasn't feeling well. I had a headache and a burning fever. I dragged around, trying to do my work as well as I could, for I was determined not to miss hearing the great teacher, Paul.

Even though we changed the meeting place to a larger room on the third floor of a public hall, it was packed full for this special occasion. We first ate bread and sipped wine, passing the loaf and cup from one believer to another. Jesus had asked us to do this as a symbol, to remind us of his body and his blood which he gave on the cross for our sins.

Then Paul began to speak. I couldn't concentrate. To my fever was added the heat from the packed bodies and the heat from the lamps sitting in every niche of the walls. It was more than I could bear.

I inched my way through the crowd to the back. There an open window made me feel I could at least breathe, although there was no breeze to fan my aching, feverish head. I felt faint, but there was no space to sit down, so I crawled up and sat on the window ledge, resting my back against the stone side.

The throbbing in my head became more intense. I knew it had been a mistake to come. I groaned under my breath as I lowered my head to rest it on my drawn-up knees.

And that's the last I remember till I awoke in the early morning hours and found myself lying on a strange bed. I blinked my eyes and saw, sitting by the bed, a young man I recognized as Timothy. My headache was gone, but my body ached all over, and as far as I could see, it was one vast bruise. I was black and blue and stiff from head to toe.

"What happened?" I croaked.

"What do you remember?" asked Timothy.

I told him of my sickness. "The last I remember is resting my head on my knees in the window," I finished.

"Well, apparently you slept for a while. At midnight when Paul was still speaking, shouts came from the back of the room. Someone called out that you had fallen from the window. Several of those near the door raced down the stairs, and then one came panting back up to tell us that you were dead."

"Dead?" I stared at him.

"You weren't breathing, at any rate. The shock of hitting the ground apparently knocked the breath out of you and stopped your heart. Paul quickly left the room and went down to you. I went with him. He pulled you up and squeezed you in his arms several times.

"Then Paul said, 'Don't be afraid. His life is still in him.' And you began breathing again! A couple of others and I carried you here to this believer's house, where we've been lodging. I've been with you, waiting for you to regain consciousness. You have no broken bones. Luke, our doctor, says that was probably because you were asleep and relaxed when you fell."

"I feel so embarrassed and stupid to have caused all this commotion," I muttered. "I had wanted so much to hear Paul's teaching. I hope I can at least thank him for saving my life, although I certainly don't want to bother him. Is he sleeping here, too?"

Timothy laughed. "He's still at the hall, talking! I

dare say you're not the only one who fell asleep during the night."

Timothy and the others left at dawn by ship for Assos. Paul wasn't finished talking yet, so he left an hour or so later, walking the few miles by land to rejoin the ship at Assos. The land route was a short-cut and by walking, he could have a few more hours to talk with the Troas church leaders, who accompanied him as far as the ship.

I did get to thank him, when he stuck his head in the door before he left, to see how I was. And then I heard him, still talking, of course, as he went out the door and down the road toward Assos.

11

Uncle Saul

by Benjamin of Tarsus

Benjamin isn't my real name, but you'll need to excuse me for writing anonymously. The events in which I took part aren't far in the past, so it would still be dangerous if others knew my relationship to Paul (or Saul, as we call him in the family).

I hadn't known my uncle very well. I was just a young boy when he had come back to Tarsus after many years away. I understood little of what went on then. I only knew that our happy life in Grandfather's house became unhappy.

Grandmother cried a lot, and Grandfather stormed around and never played with me anymore. Mother was upset and tried to find a way to make peace between her parents and her older brother, as she later explained to me.

"So, it's all been for nothing, Saul!" shouted Grandfather. "The years and money we spent on your education with the best rabbis in Jerusalem, the reports I got of your brilliance at your studies and the possibilities for your future!

"Now, here you are—over forty, hated by our leaders in Jerusalem, unable to use your great learning in the temple or in the Sanhedrin, no wife or family, no money. You top it all off by coming back here and stirring up the whole city against your family with some outlandish ideas you say came to you from God! I'll have no part of it, nor of you either, if you keep on in this way!"

"I must speak of what I know," said my uncle, trying to be patient, but he was as fiery-tempered as his father. "I must do as God wants. I'm not *trying* to cause trouble."

They couldn't agree. Mother said it was because they were too much alike. So Saul moved out of the house, but still sometimes came cautiously for visits with Grandmother and Mother. He never noticed me much, but then neither did my other uncle, Mother's younger brother: Ezra was too full of his own importance.

"You prig!" I heard Mother say to Uncle Ezra one time. "Are you happy now that you've become Father's heir? You had to tittle-tattle everything you heard about Saul. And probably exaggerated it all, too!"

Ezra simply grinned and shrugged his shoulders.

After a few years, a man named Barnabas showed up and had some vigorous conversation with Uncle Saul. They left Tarsus together, headed for Syria, as I overheard. We didn't see Uncle Saul again, but we heard of him from time to time.

There was a group of people in Tarsus whom Uncle Saul had gathered together, people who believed the things he had taught about the Messiah, Jesus of Nazareth. Mother had a friend who was one of them and who let her know when they had any news of Uncle Saul.

He was traveling about, teaching and preaching what he called the good news, and establishing groups of those who believed. Everywhere he went he met opposition, much as he had here.

Then when I was thirteen years old, my grandfather decided to send my mother and me off to Jerusalem so I could get a good religious education. Uncle Ezra, of course, opposed spending any family money on me, but Grandfather was firm. I think he wanted someone in the family to be a religious scholar. That might help to cover what he considered to be the dishonor brought by Uncle Saul.

I haven't mentioned my father. In fact, I don't remember him. He had divorced my mother soon after my birth. Through Grandfather's influence, she was allowed to bring me with her when she returned to her parents' home.

I don't think I'm a great intellectual, like my Uncle Saul is. The more I studied, the more confused I felt. The beauty of the temple, the stately rituals of prayers and offerings, the revered ancient scrolls and their teachings, the striving for goodness by the most religious—these things attracted me.

But then I would also see contradictions. According to the prophet Isaiah, God said, "My house shall be called a house of prayer for all peoples." But I saw signs in the temple forbidding Gentiles to enter the inner courts on pain of death. And I thought, *Isn't my uncle doing what's right? He's taking God to those "peoples" that many of us despise and try to keep away from the temple.*

We students studied God's great commandments in the scrolls, "Love the Lord your God. . . . Serve him only." But we spent most of our time ignoring these great laws, concentrating instead on the mass of traditions and rules which scholars had added in their interpretations throughout the centuries. These were not written, but we learned to recite them in our classes.

For instance, one of the many Sabbath regulations was supposed to be based on the great commandment which God gave through Moses, "Remember the Sabbath Day, and keep it holy." I was surprised to learn that the rabbis said, "You shall not look in a mirror on the Sabbath."

This rule came into being because of one of the main Sabbath-keeping laws passed down from Moses: "On the seventh day you shall rest; even in plowing time and in harvest time you shall rest." With some nimble thinking, the rabbis connected harvesting and looking in a mirror: "If you look into a mirror on the Sabbath, you may see a gray hair, and you may pluck it out. This is harvesting."

And so it went, tradition upon tradition upon tradition, until we almost lost sight of the great purposes of the law.

I secretly began to go to some of the meetings of those who believed in Jesus as Messiah. There I heard how he had once driven out from the temple those who desecrated it by buying and selling in its courtyard.

I also heard how Jesus had discarded unnecessary Sabbath rules and healed the sick on the Sabbath. His disciples had even plucked some grain to eat one Sabbath—harvesting! And Jesus defended them: "God made the Sabbath for the people, not the people for the Sabbath." To me, such words were like rain on thirsty soil.

So I studied with the rabbis, to please my family. But I also learned the words and teachings of Jesus. They gave meaning to the laws of God which otherwise were often buried under dead traditions.

From time to time I heard of Uncle Saul when reports came to the Jesus-believers. Some of them were glad to hear of all the "peoples" who believed through Paul's work. Others were so insulated by the traditions that they had absorbed from little up. They questioned if any non-Jews could be part of God's people without also keeping the laws and traditions of the rabbis.

I shared with my mother all I was learning and thinking. She understood, but she was worried. "Oh, my son, you must believe what you must believe. But if you follow the way of the Jesus-people, we would never be able to return to Tarsus. It would kill your grandfather."

I was troubled, too. "I know, Mother. I haven't decided. But their beliefs seem right. I'm very drawn to them."

"You're still young," she said. "You have more years of study. Don't decide yet."

And so I continued leading a double life. By day I endured my studies with the scribes and teachers. In the evenings, I attended meetings of Jesus-believers. There I listened, but stayed aloof, not sharing my thoughts or even my name. They only knew I was a student and probably feared that I was a spy for the temple leaders who opposed them. So they left me alone.

Then one day I was sitting with my group at the temple, studying the traditions which had evolved from Ezra the scribe during the restoration of our people from Babylon. Our teacher suddenly declared, "It's these sacred traditions which some are trying to overthrow! A renegade Pharisee has arrived in Jerusalem.

"At one time he was a student such as you! But he has forsaken our God and our traditions. He has taken the Jesus heresies all over the world. Some of our faithful ones have arrived from Ephesus to warn us. We must be alert. They say his purpose for coming is to desecrate the temple!"

I shivered at the hate sparking from his eyes. *Could he be talking about my uncle?* I wondered.

That night at the meeting of believers in Jesus, I listened carefully for news. Nothing was said publicly, but I overheard enough to know that it *was* my uncle Saul, and that he would be meeting with the elders the next afternoon at the home of James, the chief elder.

I also went there and was able to persuade the doorkeeper to let me stand inside the gate. There I waited for the meeting to end. After several hours, a group of men came out. I at once knew which one he was, though I hadn't seen him since I was six years old.

I gathered together my courage and went up to the group. "Excuse me, sir. I think you are my uncle Saul?"

He stared at me, then smiled. "Can it be Benjamin?"

To the others he said, "My sister's child, whom I

108

haven't seen since he was a youngster in Tarsus."

Then he put his arm around my shoulder. "And what are you doing in Jerusalem?"

I told him, then added, "Mother doesn't know yet that you're here. Please, won't you come and visit us? I know she'll want to see you."

"I'll come tonight," he said.

"Be careful," said one of his friends. "You don't want to endanger. . . ."

"I know, I know," he said. "I'll go quietly and stick to the shadows."

Then I gave him instructions on how to find our home.

I hadn't wanted to tell Mother until I knew for sure it was her brother—and until I knew he'd be able and willing to see us. She was thrilled. And in the few hours she had before he arrived, she began to prepare what she said had been some of his favorite foods when they were young together. She probably wasn't aware of the threats and hatred which were swirling around him. And I didn't tell her.

Two of his traveling companions came with him—a doctor named Luke, and Trophimus, a Greek believer from Ephesus. The first part of the evening passed in laughing and eating and reminiscing. Then, as he was questioning me about my studies, I told him what the rabbi had said about him.

"Oh, Saul, they're plotting against you!" my mother cried out.

He shrugged. "It's possible, but by now, I'm used to it."

Luke said, "On our way to Jerusalem, in several cities prophets warned Saul that trouble was waiting for him here, but he insisted on coming!"

"Now you see one reason why it was good that I came!" he replied. "My sister and nephew are here, though I didn't know it. I don't want trouble. I'll avoid it if I can. That's why I'm taking the advice of the elders of the church here and sponsoring four men in fulfilling their vows in the temple. We hope this will show my enemies that I'm not trying to turn our Jewish people away from the law. Perhaps it will help.

"Trophimus," he said to his friend, "you'd better not be too noticeable around the city, if those people from Ephesus that Benjamin mentioned are the ones I think they are."

"Agreed," he said. "The atmosphere in this city is tense enough already. Far be it from me to show my Greek face around and stir things up further!"

"Now, when are you going to decide about the Savior?" my uncle said, looking at Mother and me. "You've known about him for many years now, Sister, and Benjamin has learned much here. It would give me great joy to have some of my own family know Jesus as their Lord. Not to mention the joy *you* would have."

"Yes, and the joy our parents would have?" said Mother with a bitter smile.

He sighed. "In the Lord, you would have a new family. There would be losses, yes. I lost everything, as you know, but I consider it as rubbish compared to what I have gained in the Lord."

"I'm collecting some of the words of Jesus from those who knew him," said Luke. "Here's one of his sayings on this subject: 'Whoever comes to me and does not hate father and mother, wife and children, brothers and sisters, and even life itself, cannot be my disciple. . . . None of you can become my disciple if you do not give up all your possessions.' "

"So, my friend," said my uncle to Luke, "why did you try so often to persuade me not to come to Jerusalem? I'm only following the words of the Lord!"

It was late when they left. He kissed my mother and said, "I won't come back again, Sister, unless things go differently than I expect. It'll be better for you. The grace of our Lord be with you."

The next days much of the talk among the students and teachers was of Paul and the people who had come with him to Jerusalem. I mostly kept quiet, except for a few occasions. Sometimes I could safely raise a question about the false information that was circulating, or I could insert some truth into the mass of rumors flying about. I had the idea it was good for me to listen and gather information which might be helpful to my uncle. If I spoke up boldly and made people suspicious of me, they'd limit what they said in my presence.

About a week after we had seen my uncle, I was sitting with Rabbi Samuel and some other students on Solomon's Porch, an outer area of the temple. We heard shouting and the sound of people running, so we scrambled to our feet and ran, too. The mass of people was already too big for us to see what was happening.

"What is it? What's going on?" we cried.

"It's that Paul!" someone yelled. "He's brought a Gentile into the temple! He's defiled the temple! They're going to kill him now! Serves him right!"

I was caught, unable to get closer, unable to move back. I feared some of us would be killed in the crush of the roaring, maddened crowd.

Then there was a cry: "Give way! Give way!" Bodies were being shoved aside, crushed into places where there was no room for them. Roman soldiers forced their way through, intent on stopping the riot by finding its cause. They were from the Antonia Fortress overlooking the temple.

Finally the soldiers reached Paul at the center of the tumult. The tribune or commander of the soldiers could understand nothing from the crowd. Voices were shouting all kinds of accusations, in languages the Romans did not know. So the tribune decided that the best thing to do was to arrest the one who seemed to be the cause of the riot and remove him from the temple area.

The crowd was again forced back by the muscular soldiers with their drawn swords. They passed near me, and I saw in their midst my uncle Saul. Alongside the soldiers, he seemed small and old. His arms were chained to guards on each side of him, as if he were the dangerous one!

Others who witnessed the next events have doubtless reported them. I wasn't near enough to see what happened myself, but they say he got permission to speak to the mob from the steps leading up to the fortress. They listened at first, but then became angrier than ever when he told of his mission to the Gentiles. The tribune decided to imprison him for the night and bring him before the Jewish court (the Sanhedrin) in the morning.

The next day in the Sanhedrin, a fierce dispute broke out between two groups on the court—the Sadducees and the Pharisees. They would have torn Paul to pieces between them if the tribune hadn't once again stepped in to save him.

I dare not tell, even yet, how I learned of the plot that was hatched that night against my uncle. My life and that of others would be quickly ended if it were known. I learned that forty of his most rabid enemies had vowed neither to eat nor drink till he was dead.

They plotted with the Sanhedrin: "Call another meeting for tomorrow, and tell the tribune you need to see Paul for more questioning. We'll lie in wait and see that he never arrives at the council chamber from the fortress. Though some of us may die at the hands of the soldiers protecting him, you can be sure he will die with us!"

I took off my student clothing and dressed like a simple country boy. Then I went to the fortress and asked to see the prisoner, Paul. I was surprised that they let me in so easily, but by then they had learned that he was a Roman citizen and that he wasn't dangerous. I found him, no longer bound by chains, but surrounded by soldiers, for his own protection.

He looked surprised to see me, but his eyes lit up. Quickly I told him of the plot and of the forty waiting assassins.

I almost expected him to shrug his shoulders again at the danger. Instead he said, "Last night the Lord came to me and said that my time isn't up yet. I'm to be his witness in Rome, as I have been in Jerusalem and beyond. So, we mustn't let these plotters get rid of me. Thank you, Benjamin."

Then he called to his chief guard, a centurion, and said, "Take this boy to the tribune. He has something important to tell him."

113

So I was taken further into the fortress, into the tribune's private quarters.

"The prisoner has asked me to bring this boy and his information to you, sir," said the centurion.

The tribune looked me over. "You have something of the look of this man, Paul," he observed.

"He's my uncle, " I replied. "I've learned of a plot against him."

We went to the far end of the room where I quietly told him of the assassination plans.

"You've done well to come. I shall see to it that your uncle leaves here tonight, under guard, to go to Caesarea, to Governor Felix. I don't understand the hatreds of your religious quarrels, but my duty is to keep the peace of this city. And that's what I intend to do.

"Be sure you let no one know what you've told me, if you value your own life as well as your uncle's."

That night my uncle escaped from his enemies, although he remained in prison for several years.

Sometimes I laugh to myself as I think of his forty enemies, deprived of their prey and forced to break their solemn vows! At least I've never heard of any of them dying of hunger or thirst because they hadn't succeeded in killing Paul! In a way they helped me. Because of their insane and illogical hatred, I at last decided for the Lord.

12

Neither a Murderer
nor a God

by Drusilla of Malta

Our island isn't very large. From anywhere on it, you
can see the Great Sea. Sometimes it's deep blue with
gentle warm waves lapping the sandy side of the bay.
Sometimes it's gray with mighty waves hurling themselves against the rocks on the other side of the bay.

The sea can give us food to eat and coolness for our
bodies when the sun is hot. It also harbors poisonous
stingrays and sharp-toothed piranha, and it can be the
source of destroying winds. But friendly or unfriendly,
the sea is our constant companion.

Our ancestors, according to the old stories, came
here many generations ago, traveling on their ships
from the far eastern end of the Great Sea. After a long
voyage, they reached the western end. They settled in

many places in and along the sea, and they engaged in much commerce and trade from one end to the other.

Most of us here still live from the sea. We fish or own boats or work on the Roman ships. Often we provide supplies and services for the ships which stop at our port of Valletta.

Our small bay is used by only a few local boats. A submerged sandbar in the middle means that only light boats, manned by people who know the waters, can safely get to the sandy beach.

The events I want to tell you about happened early one winter after the ships had stopped their voyages and taken shelter. From then on, the weather becomes too unpredictable, and fierce storms sweep across the waters.

For the previous two weeks, one of these storms had been raging, a worse storm than even my father had ever seen before. We didn't leave the house. The wind was too strong, and occasionally a wave would fling itself as far as our doorstep.

The storm clouds were so dark and the rain so torrential, it was sometimes hard to tell if it was night or day. Then, in the middle of the fourteenth night, the wind died down and its shrieking decreased.

When the sky was just beginning to turn gray in the east, my father went out to have a look around and to see what damage had been done. He soon rushed back into the house, excited.

"Drusilla! There's a ship at the entrance to the bay! From what I can see, it looks like it will try to come in!"

Mother and I quickly pulled on our clothes and hurried outside. I limped along as fast I could, my shorter leg making me hobble behind. The sky was lightening,

116

and I could see the large vessel heaving on the waves. One of the Roman grain ships, it looked like. Its deck was crowded with people looking toward shore.

Then the crew raised their foresail, pulled up their anchor, and the ship suddenly began moving toward us. There was no way to warn them of the shoal that lay waiting to destroy the ship. On it moved till it ground its way to a halt on the sandbank. Its timbers seemed to shudder and groan from the impact, and the ship, already battered from two weeks of storm, began to fall apart before our eyes.

"They'll have to abandon ship quickly and try to make it to shore," said Father. "The waves aren't as high here as out beyond the bay. Maybe some will make it."

"Look, Father!" I cried. "There are Roman soldiers on board, with prisoners chained to them. They've got swords—they're going to kill the prisoners so none will escape!"

Across the water, we heard a shouted command, and the soldiers sheathed their swords and instead began to unchain the prisoners. How strange!

The ship was breaking apart fast, its stern already sinking. Men were jumping into the water. Those who could swim were fighting their way through the waves. Others grabbed pieces of floating debris and held on, paddling their legs. Some were too exhausted for that, and barely held on to pieces of the ship while the incoming tide brought them toward shore.

"Looks like most of them are going to make it!" Father shouted. By then our neighbors had come out, too, and were looking on. The wind was cold, and the rain was beginning again, not the pounding rain of the storm, but rain with a dripping, penetrating chill.

"Let's get a fire going," my father called. "These folks are going to be cold to the bone after being in that water. and they'll be half dead from coming through that storm."

"Where are we going to find enough dry wood?" complained one man.

"You know you've got some stored up. Get a move on!" Father urged.

Everyone brought some of their kindling, and we younger ones went to the wooded area where the trees were dense enough that we could find partially dry brush underneath.

By the time I dragged myself back with an armful, most of the men from the ship were ashore and were gathered around the fire, shivering and shaking from cold and shock.

I threw my contribution on the fire. "I wonder if many drowned," I said aloud to myself.

A man standing by me answered, "No one has drowned. All 276 of us have come safely to shore, just as God told me it would happen!"

What did he mean? I looked at him. He was a short, oldish man, still dripping wet, but he seemed to have undampened enthusiasm and energy.

"An excellent idea, this fire," he said. "Where did you get that brush? I'll help gather some. We should keep the fire going awhile yet."

I pointed to the nearby woods. He hurried away, joined by a few of the other shipwrecked men, and soon he was back with an armload of sticks. As he threw them onto the fire, a viper hidden among the sticks crawled out and struck his hand. There it hung, its fangs embedded.

118

What a pity! I thought. *To survive a shipwreck and then to die from a snakebite.*

He didn't seem concerned, but shook his hand until the viper let loose and dropped into the fire. Maybe he didn't know how deadly this kind of viper was!

The people nearby, our neighbors, were saying to each other in our language, "He's one of the prisoners. See the cuffs on his arms? No doubt he's a murderer. Though he escaped from the sea, he hasn't escaped judgment. Now he'll die."

If he noticed the strange way people were looking at him, he didn't let on. We kept watching. The bite of this viper could make a person swell up from the venom and die, or it could bring on a sudden fainting spasm and death. Either way, death was sure and quick. But *nothing* happened to him. Nothing at all.

After twenty minutes or so, the people began murmuring again. This time the whispers were just the opposite: "We were wrong! He must be a god! He's still well! One of the gods has come to us!"

I was standing away from the fire to give space for the people from the ship. This man came to me and said in Greek, "What are your friends muttering about me? I don't know your Phoenician dialect."

I told him what they had said.

"And what do you think?" he asked me.

"I don't think you're a murderer, although you are a prisoner. And I don't think you're a god, because you talked about what a god had told you."

"You're right," he said. "I'm a man, and my name is Paul."

"My name is Drusilla," I responded.

Before I could find out more about him, Publius, the

leading man in our area, came to invite the important people from the ship to his house. He also helped to organize guides to take the others to the port city to find lodging in the inns. It would be several months before the weather would be good enough for the sea traffic to begin moving again. Paul, though a prisoner, went with those going to the house of Publius.

Our island is small enough so that we all know each other, and our conversation is often about the affairs of our neighbors. Naturally what the newcomers did and said added much interest to the usually dull winter gossip. Of special interest was Paul, the man some thought might be a god.

Later Paul became even more the topic of conversation. The rumor spread that on his arrival at the home of Publius, he had immediately performed another miracle. He healed the father of Publius, who had been wasting away from dysentery. This continual running of the bowels is a common illness, but if people don't get over it, they will die from its weakening effects.

After that, from all directions people began bringing the sick to Publius's house, and a few days later, to the inn to which Paul and his friends moved for the rest of the winter. Many were cured. Miracles? I didn't know.

Some said that one of Paul's companions was a well-known physician, and that it was he who made the people well. But besides the dysenteries and common fevers and spotted fevers, I began to hear of broken bones quickly healed and of sick minds freed from evil spirits.

Then the question, which had always been in the back of my mind, began pushing its way forward.

120

Could this man, with his strange powers, perhaps heal my withered leg?

The question came with more insistence. *Why not at least try? What could I lose by asking? And think of the possible gain!*

It would be wonderful to be able to walk like others—with them instead of lagging behind. To run, to dance with the other girls. To be pretty enough so that in the future, my parents could find a husband for me. At last I told my parents what was on my mind.

"Dear Drusilla," said my father, "your mother and I have spoken of this very thing. We'll take you to him. We'll take what silver coins we have, and the young sheep for offering and payment. Perhaps he'll be willing to help you or to ask his gods to help you."

So we went to Valletta, I riding the neighbor's donkey so as not to have to walk that distance. I was thinking as I bounced along, "Perhaps . . . coming back, I'll be able to walk like everyone else."

We came to the inn where Paul and his friends were staying. At first we thought we wouldn't even be able to see him.

"He's ill," said the innkeeper, "but I'll tell him who's here."

The healer—ill! That wasn't a good omen. The innkeeper returned to tell us to enter. He said Paul remembered us from the morning of the shipwreck.

Paul was sitting on his bed, a cloth tied around his head, and he looked weary and pale. He wasn't alone in the room. With him was one of his friends and a soldier-guard.

My father bowed, presented his gifts, and said, "We have heard, sir, of your many kindnesses to our people.

Many have been made well from their diseases because you are, as some say, one of the gods, or as others say, a friend of the gods. We ask your help for our daughter, Drusilla, whom the gods have for some reason punished by causing her to be born with a withered leg. Can you not implore them for her healing?"

Paul gazed at us for awhile. "I'm not a god nor a friend of the gods. I am a servant of the one true God, Creator of the earth and the heavens. Sometimes it has been God's will to use me to do miraculous healings. At other times he has healed through my friend Luke's medicines and wisdom. And sometimes God lets a sickness or infirmity continue.

"I myself have an infirmity, as you can see. At times I have such severe headaches that I cannot move for several days. I'm just getting over one of these. I've asked God to heal me. I've asked several times, but he hasn't. Instead, he told me, 'My grace is sufficient for you. My power is made perfect in your weakness.'

"Sometimes God protects me, as from the venom of the poisonous snake. But other times, I have been beaten and stoned and hounded from one place to another because of doing God's work."

I wondered, *What does all this mean? Isn't he going to heal me?*

"I remember your daughter," he went on, "and how she was busy helping us poor people who were half-drowned—in spite of her handicap. She's becoming a strong person in spite of her weakness, perhaps even because of it.

"What she and you need most is the inner healing which God gives those who believe in him. Then he gives them spiritual strength which is more important than physical strength."

"You mean my leg won't be healed?"

"I mean you can be healed in a way that's even better than having a healthy leg."

My father said, "We're simple people. I'm not sure of your meaning, but I'd like to understand better."

Paul talked more about this Creator God and his son, Jesus, and we listened. Meanwhile, Doctor Luke took the sandal from my left foot. With some scraps of leather, he cut and fashioned extra pieces of leather the same size and shape as the sole of my sandal. While Paul continued to talk, he himself stitched these pieces onto the bottom of my sandal.

"I'm a tentmaker too, you know, so I'm skilled at sewing such heavy materials," he said. In the end I had a sandal whose sole was much thicker than the sole of my other sandal. This was to lengthen my short leg and give me better balance in walking! When I tried it out there in the room, it was awkward at first, but soon I could cross the room with only a slight imbalance.

Luke also showed Mother and me how to rub my leg, and he instructed us on exercises to stretch and strengthen it. This wouldn't lengthen it, he said, but it would help to keep it from shrinking more or becoming more rigid.

Paul invited us to meet with them and some others from our island who were learning about God. We did, but it was all new and strange to us, and we couldn't go to Valletta often. When the sailing season began again, our new friends left to continue on their way to Rome.

When we went to town, we kept meeting with the believers in the Creator God. After a time I realized that I had the inside healing of mind and spirit that Paul had talked about.

I've also experienced a degree of physical healing, though not in the way I had at first hoped for. I can walk almost normally, with my special shoe. Because my handicap is no longer so important in my mind, because I forget about it, so do others. And my circle of friends, boys as well as girls, is growing.

Bible and Song

Bible Texts Behind These Stories

Preface. Luke 1:1-4; Acts 1:1-5

Chapter 1. Luke 10:38-42; 24:50-53; John 11; 12:1-19; Acts 2; 5:17-23; 6:1-6; 7:1—8:3.

Chapter 2. Acts 9:1-25; 22:1-11; 26:9-18

Chapter 3. Acts 13:4-12.

Chapter 4. Acts 13:13-52; 14:1-23; 16:1-3; 1 Timothy 5:23; 2 Timothy 1:5-7; 3:14-15.

Chapter 5. Acts 16:6-15; Philippians 4:2-3.

Chapter 6. Acts 16:16-24; Philippians 4:2-3.

Chapter 7. Acts 16:19-40; Philippians 4:3, 14-20.

Chapter 8. Acts 18:1-10; Romans 16:3-5; 1 Corinthians 16:19; 2 Timothy 4:19; Romans 9:1-5; 10:1-21; 1 Corinthians 7; Galatians 3:28; Ephesians 4:4-6; Philippians 4:11-12.

Chapter 9. Acts 19:8-20.

Chapter 10. Acts 20:1-14.

Chapter 11. Acts 21:17—23:24; Luke 14:26, 33.

Chapter 12. Acts 27:1—28:11; 2 Corinthians 12:7-9.

God Loves Us

God loves us, He's our Sav - ior, God
God loves you, loves each per - son. God

loves us. In him we live. God loves us thru his
loves you tho you sin. God loves you. Won't you

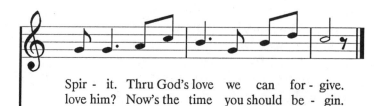

Spir - it. Thru God's love we can for - give.
love him? Now's the time you should be - gin.

The Author

Marian Hostetler teaches English as a foreign language for the Eastern Mennonite Board of Missions in a secondary school in Djibouti, a small African country bordered by Ethiopia, Somalia, and the Red Sea.

This Orrville, Ohio, native has also spent major blocks of time teaching in Algeria with Mennonite Board of Missions (1961-70) and in Indiana at Concord Schools of Elkhart (1970-88).

Most of her previous Herald Press books are based on overseas experiences: *African Adventure, Journey to Jerusalem, Fear in Algeria,* and *They Loved Their Enemies.* Two of her volumes take place in the United States: *Secret in the City* and *Mystery at the Mall.*

Some of her books have been translated into other languages: Finnish, French, German, Portuguese, and Spanish.

We Knew Paul comes out of her interest in the Bible, her study of it, and her experience of its truth.

She says, "The first two books I ever wrote were biblical novels—never published. So I'm excited about having these stories of Paul appear. I hope many people will read them and feel that Paul and his time have become more real and understandable to them."

Besides teaching and writing, Hostetler enjoys reading, painting, and trying to keep from melting while living in what some say is the world's hottest country. In Djibouti she worships with the small French-speaking Protestant Church and with other English-speaking Christians. She also maintains ties with Belmont Mennonite Church, Elkhart, Indiana, through the tapes they send of their weekly worship services.